People Follow Me

Unlocking Effective Leadership

By

Nico D'Alessandro

Revision 1: 5/9/2024

Dedication:

I dedicate this book to my incredibly supportive, brilliant, and amazing wife, Kally, and my two outstanding, athletic, and wonderful children, Antonio and Vinny. Everything I do in life is for you. Family is everything.

I also dedicate this book to all the great leaders I have had or had the pleasure of working with throughout my career. I have learned a tremendous amount from all of you and continue to seek ways to pay it forward by sharing my insights, experiences and lessons learned. Together we are shaping the future.

Table of Contents

I. Introduction 7
   A. Setting the Stage: The Evolving Landscape of Leadership 9
   B. The Importance of Strong Leadership in Today's World 12
   C. The Negative Impact from a Weak or Ineffective leadership 14

II. The Essence of Leadership 17
   A. What It Means to Lead 17
   B. The Role of Leadership in Personal & Professional Development 19

III. Characteristics of Effective Leaders 23
   A. Ambition 26
   B. Respect 27
   C. Charisma 28
   D. Courage 30
   E. Positivity 31

IV. Understanding Yourself as a Leader 35
   A. The Foundation of Leadership 36
   B. Understand your Own Strengths and Weaknesses 38
   C. Leading with Integrity and Authenticity 39
   D. Leverage your Life Experiences 40
   E. Humor in Leadership 42

V. Tailoring Your Leadership Approach 45
   A. Recognizing Individual Differences Amongst Your Team 47
   B. Adapting Your Leadership Style to Different Situations 49

VI. Building High-Performing Teams 53
   A. Inspiring Others to Follow 53
   B. Team Roles and Group Dynamics 55

    C. The Art of Listening 56

    D. Fostering a Culture of Collaboration and Innovation.................... 57

    E. Delicate Balance of Management vs Micromanagement 59

    F. Get Friendly, But Not Too Friendly 61

    G. Strength of the Leader is Dependent on the Strength of the Team 62

    H. The Challenge of Managing Remote Teams 63

VII. Leading Through Change, Uncertainty and Transformation 67

    A. The Challenges of Leading in Turbulent Times............................. 68

    B. Strategies for Leading Change Effectively & Building Resilience .. 69

    C. Conflict Resolution 71

VIII. Emotional Intelligence in Leadership... 73

    A. Recognizing and Managing Emotions.. 74

    B. Connecting with Others on a Human Level 75

    C. Effectiveness of Strong Team Camaraderie 77

    D. Bouncing Back from Adversity.. 79

IX.   Decision-Making and Problem-Solving 81

    A. Making Informed Decisions for Long-Term Success...................... 82

    B. Adapting to Change and Leading Through Challenges.................. 84

    C. Turning Setbacks into Opportunities for Growth 87

X.   The Diversity of Leadership Styles 89

    A. The Correlation Between Successful Athletes and Strong Leadership... 98

XI.   Leadership Philosophy... 101

    A. Building Trust and Credibility.. 102

    B. Inspiring Others to Align with a Shared Vision and Mission........ 104

  C. Balancing Stakeholder Interests and Team Moral 106

  D. Your Role as an Ethical Leader 107

XII. Cultivating Leadership at Every Level... 109

  A. Delegating Authority and Encouraging Ownership..................... 109

  B. Developing the Next Generation of Leaders 111

  C. Role Modeling the Behaviors You Want to See in Others 113

XIII. Sustaining Leadership Excellence... 115

  A. Investing in Your Development as a Leader 116

  B. Building a Leadership Development Plan.................................... 117

  C. Surround Yourself with Successful Mentors and Peers............... 119

  D. Seeking Feedback and Mentoring 121

XIV. Leaving a Legacy 123

  A. The Power of Purpose-Driven Leadership................................... 124

  B. Impact of Advocacy in your community and how it Affects Your Companies Reputation 125

  C. Unleash the Leader Within You... 126

  D. Speaking to the masses... 127

XV. Conclusion... 131

  A. Final Thoughts on the Dynamic Nature of Leadership................ 131

  B. Empowering Readers to Embrace Their Leadership Journey...... 132

About the Author 134

Bold lettering = Indicates an impactful statement that you should take note of, highlight or read multiple times

I. Introduction

Leadership is often portrayed as a singular, uniform concept, with a set of traits and behaviors that define what it means to be a leader. However, the reality is far more complex. In this book, we will explore why leadership is not one size fits all and examine the intricacies of leadership development.

It is essential to recognize that leadership is inherently relative. **Different situations require different approaches to leadership, and what may be effective in one scenario may not necessarily work in another.** For example, a crisis may call for a directive and authoritative leadership style to provide clarity and decisiveness, while a creative project may benefit from a more collaborative and empowering approach that encourages innovation. The ability to adapt one's leadership style to suit the needs of the situation is a hallmark of effective leadership.

Leadership is deeply influenced by the individuals involved, both the leaders and the followers. All leaders come from diverse backgrounds and possess a wide range of personality traits, skills, and experiences. Likewise, followers also have their own unique preferences, expectations, and motivations. Effective leadership requires an understanding of these individual differences and the ability to tailor one's approach accordingly to accomplish the task at hand. What works for one team or organization may not necessarily work for another, highlighting the importance of flexibility and adaptability in leadership.

It is reasonable for an organization to expect productivity out of a team, but it is unreasonable for an organization to expect that path to success to be the same for every team. The variable in the equation of team success is the unique experiences and perspectives of the leader and the team.

Leadership is not solely about individual leaders but also about the collective leadership within an organization. In complex and rapidly changing environments, distributed leadership models are becoming increasingly prevalent, where leadership is shared among multiple individuals rather than concentrated in a single figurehead. This approach recognizes that leadership can emerge from any level of the organization and encourages collaboration, empowerment, and accountability among team members.

The effectiveness of leadership also is very dependent on the specific goals and objectives of the organization. For example, a leader who excels at driving short-term financial results may not necessarily be well-suited to lead a team through a period of organizational change or transition. Effective leadership requires a deep understanding of the organization's mission, values, and strategic priorities, as well as the ability to align individual and team efforts towards achieving them. Leaders must be able to articulate a compelling vision, inspire others to share in it, and provide the guidance and support necessary to bring it to fruition.

Leadership can't static but rather evolves over time in response to changing circumstances and experiences. Effective leaders are lifelong learners who are open to feedback, reflection, and personal growth. They continuously seek to improve their skills and expand their knowledge, adapting their approach as they gain new insights and experiences. This willingness to evolve and adapt is essential for staying relevant and effective in today's dynamic and unpredictable business environment.

What is becoming very evident, is that leadership is not one size fits all but rather a dynamic and multifaceted phenomenon that varies depending on the context, the individuals involved, and the specific goals and objectives of the organization. By embracing diversity, fostering collaboration, and continuously striving for personal and professional growth, leaders can unlock the full potential of themselves, their teams, and their organizations.

This book will serve as a guide to develop your leadership approach and skill set in a way that will be effective for just you and your organization. I can guarantee that the answers you seek in your journey of becoming a successful leader are in this book and in your soul. **It is your responsibility to connect the dots between the two.** As you read this book, open your mind to new possibilities, be curious, be vulnerable and buckle in, you're about to go on a wild ride. At the end of this ride is success and professional fulfillment.

A. Setting the Stage: The Evolving Landscape of Leadership

The landscape of leadership in the business world is undergoing profound transformation, driven by a confluence of factors including technological advancements, globalization, shifting demographics, and changing societal expectations. In this section, we will explore the evolving landscape of leadership, examining key trends and challenges shaping the way leaders operate in today's dynamic environment.

1. **Globalization**: Globalization has connected businesses and markets across borders, creating new opportunities for growth and expansion while also introducing unprecedented levels of complexity and competition. Leaders operating in a globalized world must possess a global mindset, understanding cultural nuances, geopolitical dynamics, and market trends in diverse regions. They must also be adept at building and leading multicultural teams, fostering collaboration and inclusivity across geographic boundaries.

2. **Changing Demographics**: The workforce is becoming increasingly diverse, with multiple generations working side by side and a growing emphasis on inclusion and equity. Millennials and Generation Z are bringing new values, expectations, and preferences to the workplace, challenging traditional leadership models and driving demand for more transparent, authentic, and purpose-driven leadership. Leaders must adapt their approach and communication style to accommodate the needs and aspirations of a multigenerational workforce, creating environments that foster creativity, collaboration, and personal growth.

Moreover, diversity and inclusion have become imperatives for organizational success, with research showing that diverse teams outperform homogeneous ones in terms of innovation, decision-making, and financial performance.

3. **Rapid Pace of Change**: The business landscape is characterized by constant change and disruption, driven by technological innovation, market dynamics, and shifting consumer preferences. In this volatile market, leaders must be agile and adaptable, capable of anticipating and responding to change with speed and resilience. They must foster a culture of innovation and experimentation, empowering employees to take risks and learn from failure. Also, leaders must be proactive in scanning the horizon for emerging trends and disruptions, positioning their organizations to capitalize on new opportunities and mitigate potential threats.

4. **Focus on Purpose and Values**: There is a growing recognition of the importance of purpose-driven leadership, with stakeholders increasingly demanding that businesses not only deliver financial returns but also make a positive impact on society and the environment. Leaders are expected to articulate a clear sense of purpose that inspires and motivates employees, customers, and other stakeholders. They must lead with integrity, demonstrating a commitment to ethical behavior, social responsibility, and sustainability.

5. **Emphasis on Emotional Intelligence**: Emotional intelligence (EQ) has emerged as a critical leadership competency, with research showing that it is a better predictor of success than technical skills or IQ. Leaders with high emotional intelligence are better able to understand and manage their own emotions, as well as those of others, fostering strong relationships, resolving conflicts, and inspiring trust and loyalty. In addition, emotional intelligence enables leaders to navigate complex interpersonal dynamics and motivate teams to achieve their full

potential. As such, organizations are increasingly investing in leadership development programs that focus on enhancing emotional intelligence competencies.

6. **Shift Towards Collaborative Leadership**: Traditional hierarchical leadership models are giving way to more collaborative and inclusive approaches, where leadership is distributed across teams and individuals rather than concentrated in a single leader. Collaborative leadership encourages participation, empowerment, and shared decision-making, fostering a sense of ownership and accountability among team members. Leaders must adapt to this new paradigm by relinquishing control and embracing a more facilitative role, creating environments that foster creativity, innovation, and collaboration.

7. **Importance of Learning and Development**: Lifelong learning has become essential for leaders to stay relevant and effective in today's fast-paced business environment. Leaders must continuously update their skills and knowledge, staying abreast of emerging trends, technologies, and best practices. Organizations are investing in leadership development programs that focus on building essential competencies such as communication, strategic thinking, and problem-solving, as well as fostering a growth mindset and resilience in the face of challenges.

8. **High Performance Culture**: In today's business landscape, a high-performance culture is crucial for organizations to stay competitive, agile, and customer-centric. It fosters excellence, innovation, and resilience, enabling organizations to adapt quickly to market changes and seize new opportunities. A high-performance culture also prioritizes employee engagement, talent development, and ethical leadership, driving productivity, satisfaction, and long-term success. By embracing a high-performance culture, organizations can effectively navigate the complexities of the modern business environment while delivering superior value to customers and stakeholders.

The landscape of leadership in the business world is evolving rapidly, driven by technological advancements, globalization, changing demographics, and shifting societal expectations. Effective leaders must navigate this complex terrain with agility, adaptability, and a strong sense of purpose and values. **By embracing digital transformation, fostering diversity and inclusion, cultivating emotional intelligence, and adopting collaborative and inclusive leadership approaches, leaders can thrive in today's dynamic environment and drive sustainable success for their organizations.**

B. The Importance of Strong Leadership in Today's World

Strong leadership plays a pivotal role in shaping the trajectory of organizations, communities, and societies in today's complex and interconnected world. With rapid technological advancements, globalization, and demographic shifts, the need for effective leadership has never been more critical. In this section, we will explore the importance of strong leadership in today's world and the situational leadership styles that you can adapt to the right situation.

A strong leader is not only critical, but it's necessary for driving organizational success and achieving strategic objectives. Organizations face a myriad of challenges, including technological disruption, changing market dynamics, and geopolitical uncertainties. **Organizations need to provide vision, direction, and guidance, to help their employees navigate these challenges and position their organizations for long-term success.** Leaders are needed to inspire confidence, foster innovation, and cultivate a culture of excellence, motivating employees to perform at their best and achieve both individual and collective goals. They are also adept at managing change and uncertainty, guiding their organizations through periods of transition and transformation with resilience and agility.

It is also essential to foster a positive organizational culture and to nurture employee engagement and morale. **Research has shown that employees are more likely to be engaged and committed to their work when they feel valued, supported, and inspired by their managers.** Employees also want to enjoy what they do. It is said, if you truly enjoy what you do you won't work another day in your life. They create environments where employees feel empowered to contribute their ideas, take ownership of their work, and develop their skills and potential. They foster open communication, trust, and collaboration, building strong relationships based on mutual respect and accountability. By prioritizing the well-being and development of their employees, they create a sense of purpose and belonging that drives individual and organizational performance.

In addition to driving organizational success, strong leadership is crucial for addressing pressing societal challenges and advancing the greater good. They demonstrate empathy, compassion, and ethical integrity, advocating for justice, equality, and sustainability. They collaborate with diverse stakeholders, including governments, businesses, civil society organizations, and communities, to develop holistic solutions that benefit all stakeholders. They also inspire collective action and mobilize resources to tackle these challenges, encouraging individuals and organizations to work together towards common goals.

Moreover, strong leadership is essential for fostering innovation and driving financial growth and prosperity. In today's economy, innovation is the engine of growth and competitiveness, driving productivity gains, creating new markets, and generating value for customers. They provide resources, support, and recognition for innovative ideas and initiatives, empowering employees to challenge the status quo and pursue breakthrough innovations. They also cultivate partnerships and collaborations with external stakeholders, including academia, research institutions, and the private sector, to leverage diverse expertise and resources for innovation.

Furthermore, strong leadership is crucial for promoting diversity, inclusion, and equity in today's increasingly diverse and multicultural societies. In a world characterized by demographic shifts and social change, leaders play a critical role in fostering environments where everyone feels valued, respected, and included. They actively recruit and develop diverse talent, ensuring that voices from all backgrounds are heard and represented. They advocate for equity and social justice, addressing systemic barriers and biases that perpetuate inequality and discrimination.

Leadership is essential for driving organizational success, fostering positive organizational cultures, addressing societal challenges, promoting innovation and economic growth, and advancing diversity and inclusion. The need for effective leadership has never been greater. **By cultivating strong leadership capabilities, we can unlock the full potential of individuals, organizations, driving positive change and creating a more lucrative future for all.**

C. The Negative Impact from a Weak or Ineffective leadership

Alternatively, bad leadership within an organization can unleash a cascade of detrimental consequences that permeate every facet of its operations and culture. Primarily, the absence of strong leadership diminishes clarity and direction, leaving employees adrift in uncertainty. Without a clear vision or strategic guidance, decision-making becomes erratic and reactive, hindering progress and perpetuating a sense of instability. **Morale among employees' plummets as they witness the absence of effective leadership, resulting in disengagement, decreased productivity, and high turnover rates.**

When a manager lacks the ability to inspire, motivate, and guide their team, employees may feel disconnected from the organization's mission and objectives. This disconnect can manifest in a lack of commitment to tasks, a decline in teamwork, and an overall sense of apathy towards organizational goals. As a result, the organization's performance suffers, with projects delayed, deadlines missed, and quality compromised. **Moreover, it leaves employees feeling unsupported and undervalued, leading to increased absenteeism, resentment, and eventual burnout.**

In addition to eroding morale and performance, weak or ineffective leadership can have a profound impact on the organizational culture. They play a crucial role in shaping the values, norms, and behaviors of employees, and when they fail to lead by example, it can lead to a toxic work environment characterized by mistrust, cynicism, and conflict. Without strong leadership to promote open communication, collaboration, and respect, employees may resort to backstabbing, and blame-shifting, further exacerbating dysfunction within the organization.

The absence of effective leadership can also stifle creativity, innovation, and adaptability within the organization. **They are responsible for fostering a culture of experimentation, risk-taking, and learning, but when they prioritize**

stability and control over innovation and growth, it can lead to stagnation, complacency and high turnover. Employees may hesitate to voice new ideas or challenge the status quo for fear of reprisal or ridicule, resulting in missed opportunities for improvement and growth. Furthermore, a lack of support or recognition for innovative efforts can demoralize employees and deter them from pursuing creative solutions to organizational challenges.

Bad leadership can undermine trust and confidence in the organization, both internally and externally. Employees who lack faith in their leaders may question the organization's values, integrity, and commitment to its stakeholders. This erosion of trust can lead to decreased employee loyalty, increased turnover, and difficulty attracting top talent. Moreover, external stakeholders, such as customers, shareholders, investors, and partners, may lose confidence in the organization's ability to deliver on its promises, leading to lost business opportunities, damaged relationships, and tarnished reputation.

The financial repercussions can be severe, with declining revenues, increased costs, and damaged reputation jeopardizing the organization's long-term viability. **Inefficient decision-making, poor resource allocation, and missed opportunities can lead to wasted resources, lost revenue, and decreased profitability.** The negative impact of weak leadership on employee morale, performance, and retention can result in increased recruitment and training costs, as well as decreased productivity and revenue generation. The erosion of trust and confidence in an organization can lead to lost business opportunities, decreased customer loyalty, and diminished investor confidence, further impacting the organization's bottom line.

Weak and ineffective leadership can have a profound and far-reaching impact on an organization, affecting its performance, culture, reputation, and financial health. Without strong leadership to provide vision, direction, and support, organizations may struggle to adapt to challenges, capitalize on opportunities, and maintain competitiveness in the market. **Therefore, it is *imperative* for organizations to prioritize the development and hiring of strong leaders to guide their teams to success.** Only then can organizations navigate challenges, foster innovation, and achieve sustainable growth and success in today's dynamic and competitive landscape.

Micromanagement can also have a detrimental impact on the business culture by fostering a climate of distrust, stifling creativity, and demoralizing employees. Constant scrutiny and control undermine autonomy, eroding morale and motivation among team members. This leads to decreased productivity, higher turnover rates, and increased stress levels, ultimately harming employee well-being and organizational performance. Micromanagement also inhibits innovation and problem-solving, as employees become reluctant to take initiative or propose new ideas. A micromanager creates a toxic work environment that undermines collaboration, innovation, and employee engagement, hindering the organization's growth and success.

Employees often leave their managers, not their organizations. They quit because the relationship between an employee and their manager profoundly influences their job satisfaction and overall experience at work. The leadership style of a boss significantly impacts the working environment, with employees thriving under supportive, empowering leaders and becoming disengaged or demotivated under micromanaging or unsupportive ones. Effective communication, recognition, feedback, trust, and respect are foundational to a healthy working relationship, and when these elements are lacking, employees may feel undervalued, misunderstood, or unappreciated.

Leaders who provide opportunities for growth and development, respect work-life balance, and foster a culture of trust and mutual respect are more likely to retain their employees. In contrast, managers who neglect employee development, disregard work-life balance, or create a culture of overwork may contribute to dissatisfaction and turnover. Ultimately, the quality of the relationship between an employee and their manager plays a significant role in whether employees choose to stay or leave their jobs, highlighting the critical importance of effective leadership and management at all levels of an organization.

If you're dealing with a bad leader, start by communicating your concerns to them respectfully and constructively. Seek feedback, document incidents, and explore potential solutions. Reach out to HR, a mentor, or a trusted colleague for support and advice. Focus on maintaining professionalism and performing your job to the best of your ability. If efforts to address the situation directly prove unsuccessful and the working environment becomes intolerable, consider exploring other options such as transferring departments or seeking opportunities elsewhere. Remember to prioritize your well-being and career development as you navigate the challenges posed by a bad leader.

II. The Essence of Leadership

A. What It Means to Lead

At its core, being a leader entails more than just holding a position of authority or wielding power; it involves inspiring and empowering others to achieve common goals and realize their full potential. A leader is someone who embodies vision, integrity, and empathy, who leads by example and inspires trust and confidence in those they lead. In this section, we will explore what it means to be a leader and the responsibilities that a good leader has for fostering a successful organization.

First and foremost, there is no set definition of a leader as there are many different types. **A leader is someone who provides or carries out the vision and direction for the organization.** They can articulate a compelling vision of the future, setting ambitious yet achievable goals that inspire and motivate others to action. They communicate this vision clearly and effectively, ensuring that all members of the organization understand their role in achieving it. They provide guidance and support, helping individuals and teams navigate obstacles and stay focused on the overarching goals. Moreover, they foster a culture of innovation and adaptability, encouraging creativity and experimentation in pursuit of the organization's vision.

A leader can also be someone who leads by example, demonstrating the values and principles that define the organization's culture through their actions. They embody integrity, honesty, and ethical behavior in all their actions and decisions, setting a positive example for others to follow. They treat others with respect and dignity, regardless of their position or background, fostering a culture of inclusivity and belonging. **They hold themselves and others accountable for their actions, recognizing both achievements and shortcomings and learning from failures to drive continuous improvement. They also foster open communication and transparency, creating an environment where trust and collaboration thrive.**

In addition to providing vision and leading by example, a leader is responsible for fostering a positive organizational culture and nurturing employee engagement and morale. They create an environment where employees feel valued, supported, and empowered to contribute their best work. They invest in the development and well-being of their team members, providing opportunities for growth, learning, and advancement. Ultimately, they foster a sense of belonging and camaraderie, building strong relationships based on trust, respect, and mutual support.

Organizations need managers to inspire and motivate their teams to achieve their full potential. They recognize and celebrate the strengths and talents of their team members, empowering them to take on new challenges and stretch beyond their comfort zones. They provide encouragement and support, instilling confidence, and self-belief in those they lead. They foster a culture of excellence and continuous learning, encouraging individuals and teams to strive for excellence and pursue personal and professional growth. **They also lead with empathy and compassion, understanding the unique needs and aspirations of their team members and providing the support and resources necessary for their success.**

They are responsible for fostering innovation and for driving organizational growth. They create a culture of innovation by encouraging creativity, experimentation, and risk-taking, and by providing resources and support for new ideas and initiatives. They also foster collaboration and cross-functional teamwork, breaking down silos and leveraging diverse perspectives and expertise to drive innovation. They encourage a growth mindset and a willingness to learn from failure, recognizing that innovation requires resilience and perseverance. They also develop strategic partnerships and alliances, both within and outside the organization, to drive growth and expand the organization's reach and impact.

A leader is also responsible for ensuring the long-term sustainability and success of the organization. **They develop and execute both short and long** term strategic plans and initiatives that align with the organization's mission, vision, and values. They anticipate and mitigate risks, proactively identifying opportunities and threats in the external environment and adapting the organization's strategy accordingly. They allocate resources effectively, prioritizing investments that will drive sustainable growth and create long-term value. They also build resilience and agility into the organization's culture and operations, ensuring that it can adapt and thrive in the face of change and uncertainty.

Most organizations are driving a culture of diversity, inclusion, and equity. Organizations recognize the importance of diversity in driving innovation, creativity, and organizational performance, and they actively recruit, develop, and retain diverse talent. A leader creates opportunities for underrepresented groups to succeed and advance within the organization, ensuring that everyone has a voice and an opportunity to contribute. They foster a culture of inclusion and belonging, where everyone feels valued, respected, and empowered to be their authentic selves. They also promote equity and social justice, advocating for fair and equitable policies and practices that promote equality of opportunity and access for all.

Ultimately, a good leader is someone who embodies integrity, empathy, and resilience, and who leads with purpose and passion to create a brighter future for all.

B. The Role of Leadership in Personal & Professional Development

A Leader's responsibility to develop their employees both professionally and personally is essential for fostering growth, engagement, and fulfillment within the organization. Firstly, on a professional level, leaders must provide opportunities for skill development and career advancement. This involves identifying individual strengths and areas for improvement, offering relevant training programs, and providing constructive feedback and coaching. By investing in their employees' professional development, leaders not only enhance their skills and competencies but also demonstrate a commitment to their long-term success and growth within the organization. This is counterintuitive because you are developing your people, so in theory, they will be better positioned to leave your team. However, although this may be the case, it's the right thing to do and will ultimately make them more productive employees. They will also be more loyal to you because of it.

Managers play a crucial role in providing mentorship and guidance to their employees. By sharing their knowledge, experience, and insights, leaders help employees navigate challenges, make informed decisions, and achieve their career goals. This mentorship can take various forms, such as one-on-one coaching sessions, shadowing them in meetings, or constantly providing feedback. Through mentorship, leaders empower their employees to overcome obstacles, build confidence, and unlock their full potential.

Furthermore, leaders have a responsibility to create a culture of continuous learning and development within the organization. This involves fostering an environment where curiosity, experimentation, and innovation are encouraged and rewarded. Leaders can facilitate learning opportunities through workshops, seminars, and conferences. **By promoting a culture of continuous learning, they enable employees to stay relevant in a rapidly changing business landscape and adapt to new challenges and opportunities.**

Managers must recognize and celebrate the achievements and contributions of their employees. By acknowledging their successes and milestones, they reinforce a sense of accomplishment and motivation among their teams. This recognition can take various forms, such as verbal praise, email praise, or performance bonuses. By showing appreciation for their employees' hard work and dedication, leaders foster a positive and supportive work environment where individuals feel valued and motivated to perform at their best.

Beyond professional development, leaders also have a responsibility to support the personal growth and personal well-being of their employees. This involves recognizing and respecting the individual needs, aspirations, and values of each team member. They can support personal development by providing opportunities for work-life balance, flexibility, and self-care. This may include offering flexible work arrangements, wellness programs, or mental health resources often provided through a company's benefit package. By prioritizing employee well-being, leaders create a supportive and inclusive work environment where individuals can thrive both personally and professionally.

Managers can also foster personal growth by encouraging employees to pursue their passions and interests outside of work. This may involve supporting employees' involvement in volunteer activities, hobbies, or community initiatives. By promoting work-life integration and providing opportunities for personal fulfillment, they demonstrate a commitment to their employees' holistic development and happiness.

The analogy "happy wife, happy life" can be adapted to describe employee productivity as "happy employee, happy results." Just as a happy spouse contributes to a harmonious and fulfilling relationship, a content and satisfied employee is more likely to contribute positively to their work environment and performance outcomes. When employees feel valued, supported, and engaged, they are motivated to put forth their best effort, collaborate effectively with colleagues, and achieve their goals. Conversely, unhappy, or disengaged employees may experience decreased productivity, morale, and job satisfaction, ultimately impacting overall performance and organizational success. Therefore, prioritizing employee well-being, recognition, and fulfillment is essential for fostering a positive work culture and maximizing productivity.

A leader's responsibility to develop their employees both professionally and personally is *essential* for fostering growth, engagement, and fulfillment within the organization. By providing opportunities for professional development, mentorship, and continuous learning, leaders empower their employees to achieve their career goals and unlock their full potential. Additionally, by supporting personal growth and well-being, they can create a positive and supportive work environment where individuals can thrive both personally and professionally. Through their commitment to employee development, they not only enhance organizational performance but also cultivate a culture of growth, loyalty, resilience, and excellence.

III. Characteristics of Effective Leaders

An effective leader can transform a business in many ways. Some focus on providing vision and strategy, others focus on shaping culture and values, fostering innovation, prioritizing employee engagement and development, while some are experts in leading change management initiatives, focusing on customer needs, and demonstrating ethical leadership through difficult situations. Most leaders are a combination of some of these focus areas.

Either way, they articulate a compelling vision for the future and develop strategic plans to achieve it, providing direction and purpose for the organization. **By promoting transparency, trust, and collaboration, the leader creates a positive work environment where employees feel valued and motivated to perform at their best.** Encouraging innovation and creativity, the leader drives continuous improvement and ensures the organization stays ahead of the competition. Prioritizing employee engagement and development, they empower individuals to reach their full potential and contribute to the organization's success. Leading change effectively, the leader navigates complexity with confidence, ensuring the organization can adapt and thrive in a rapidly changing business environment. By focusing on understanding and meeting customer needs, they drive towards customer satisfaction and loyalty. Demonstrating integrity and ethical behavior, they build trust with stakeholders, enhancing the reputation and sustainability of the business.

There are five commonly shared characteristics of effective leaders. I have also provided examples of famous leaders who embody each trait:

1. **Visionary**: Effective leaders have a clear vision of the future and can inspire others to work towards that vision. They are forward-thinking and able to see opportunities where others may only see challenges.

   A famous example of a visionary leader is Steve Jobs, co-founder of Apple Inc. Jobs had a bold vision for transforming the technology industry and creating products that would change the way people live, work, and communicate. His vision led to the development of groundbreaking products such as the Mac Computer, iPhone, iPad, and MacBook, which revolutionized multiple industries and transformed Apple into one of the most valuable companies in the world.

2. **Authenticity**: Authentic leaders are genuine and true to themselves, inspiring trust, and confidence in others. They are transparent about their values, beliefs, and intentions, and they lead with integrity and honesty.

   Oprah Winfrey, media mogul and philanthropist, is a shining example of authenticity in leadership. Throughout her career, Winfrey has remained true to her values of empathy, authenticity, and empowerment, using her platform to uplift and inspire millions of people around the world. Her authenticity and vulnerability have earned her the trust and admiration of her audience, making her one of the most authentic leaders of our time.

3. **Empathy**: Effective leaders are empathetic and compassionate, able to understand and connect with the emotions and experiences of others. They demonstrate care and concern for the well-being of their team members, fostering a sense of belonging and support.

   Howard Schultz, former CEO of Starbucks, is known for his empathetic leadership style. He prioritized employee well-being, offering healthcare benefits and stock options, and supported initiatives like tuition reimbursement. Schultz's empathy-driven decisions fostered a positive work culture and customer loyalty, shaping Starbucks into a socially responsible global brand.

4. **Resilience**: Resilient leaders can bounce back from setbacks and adversity, remaining steadfast in the face of challenges. They demonstrate perseverance and determination, never losing sight of their goals despite obstacles and setbacks.

    Elon Musk, CEO of Tesla and SpaceX, exemplifies resilience in the face of adversity. Despite setbacks and criticism, he persevered with ambitious projects like electric vehicles and space exploration. Musk's resilience is evident in his ability to overcome challenges and propel his companies towards groundbreaking achievements in technology and innovation.

5. **Empowerment**: Effective leaders empower others to achieve their full potential, providing support, guidance, and opportunities for growth and development. They delegate authority and encourage autonomy, trusting their team members to make decisions and take ownership of their work.

    Jack Ma, co-founder of Alibaba Group, is a renowned empowerment business leader. He transformed Alibaba into a global e-commerce giant, empowering millions of small businesses to thrive in the digital economy. Ma's vision, entrepreneurial spirit, and commitment to empowering entrepreneurs have revolutionized the business landscape in China and beyond.

These leaders inspire and motivate others to achieve their full potential and make a positive impact on the world. Although each leader had a completely different path on their journey to success, they all shared common traits and characteristics. Through their actions and example, they create environments where individuals and organizations can thrive and succeed. **You are on a path to success and *if* you can embrace the characteristics that are most natural to you, you can *also* find the path to success and fulfilment.**

A. Ambition

Ambition serves as a cornerstone trait for effective leadership, wielding a profound influence on both individual accomplishment and organizational triumph. At its core, ambition ignites an insatiable drive within leaders to surpass expectations and achieve their loftiest goals. This relentless pursuit of excellence propels leaders forward, infusing their every action with purpose and determination. **Ambitious leaders are not content with mediocrity; they harbor a deep-seated desire to leave an indelible mark on the world through their contributions.** This innate drive fosters a visionary leadership style, characterized by a clear and compelling vision that inspires and galvanizes others to action. They articulate bold objectives that captivate the imagination and rally teams around a shared purpose, setting the stage for transformative change and collective achievement.

Ambition also fuels innovation and growth, propelling teams to explore uncharted territories and challenge the status quo. An ambitious leader serves as a catalysts for progress, constantly seeking out new ideas, embracing change, and pushing the boundaries of what is possible. They possess an insatiable curiosity and an unwavering commitment to continuous improvement, driving innovation within their organizations and positioning them for long-term success in dynamic and ever-evolving environments. Ambition also instills resilience in leaders, enabling them to weather the storms of adversity with grace and determination. In the face of setbacks and challenges, ambitious leaders remain steadfast in their pursuit of excellence, viewing obstacles as opportunities for growth and learning rather than insurmountable barriers. Their resilience serves as a beacon of hope and inspiration for their teams, instilling confidence, and fortitude in the face of adversity.

Furthermore, ambition motivates and inspires others, creating a ripple effect of enthusiasm and determination throughout the organization. Ambitious leaders lead by example, embodying the values of hard work, dedication, and perseverance in everything they do. Their unwavering commitment to success inspires loyalty and commitment among their teams, fostering a culture of high performance and accountability. It also guides strategic decision-making, empowering leaders to anticipate future trends and make bold, visionary choices that position their organizations for sustainable growth and prosperity. Ambitious leaders are not content to merely react to change; they actively seek out opportunities to shape the future and drive positive transformation within their organizations.

Ultimately, ambition fuels the desire to leave a lasting impact and build a legacy of success and achievement. **Ambitious leaders aspire to make a meaningful difference in the world, leveraging their talents and resources to create positive change in their organizations, industries, and communities.** They are driven by a deep-seated sense of purpose and a relentless determination to realize their full potential and make a lasting mark on the world. Ambition emerges as a foundational trait for effective leadership, empowering leaders to inspire, innovate, and achieve greatness in pursuit of their goals.

If you are struggling with leadership or you have made some mistakes along the way, don't fret. Channel your ambition as a guiding light to navigate through the struggles you face. Let your relentless drive propel you forward, pushing past obstacles and setbacks with unwavering determination. **Use your ambition to fuel your resilience, knowing that every challenge is an opportunity to showcase your strength and tenacity. Set audacious goals that inspire and motivate you, pushing the boundaries of what you thought possible.** Embrace failure as a necessary step on the path to success, viewing each setback as a chance to learn, grow, and evolve. Cultivate a mindset of continuous improvement, always seeking new opportunities for growth and development. With your ambition as your compass, you have the power to overcome any obstacle and achieve greatness. So, keep striving, keep pushing, and never lose sight of the extraordinary leader you are destined to become.

B. Respect

A business leader needs to have the respect of their employees to be successful for several reasons. **Respect fosters trust and collaboration, creating a positive work environment where individuals feel valued and appreciated.** When employees respect their leader, they are more likely to trust their decisions, follow their guidance, and work together towards common goals. This leads to increased productivity, creativity, and job satisfaction within the organization.

Respect also motivates and engages employees, encouraging them to perform at their best. **When employees feel respected by their leader, they are more likely to feel motivated to go above and beyond in their work, resulting in higher levels of performance and achievement.** Additionally, respect enhances a leader's ability to influence and inspire their team members, making it easier to communicate a vision, motivate action, and drive change within the organization.

It also contributes to employee well-being and retention. **They are more likely to experience job satisfaction and loyalty, leading to reduced turnover and increased retention rates.** These leaders prioritize the development and well-being of their employees, creating a supportive and inclusive work environment where individuals can thrive.

Respect is essential for building strong relationships, fostering trust and collaboration, motivating employees, and driving organizational success. Leaders who earn the respect of their employees are better positioned to inspire and empower their teams, achieve their business objectives, and create a positive and productive work culture.

One of the most respected business leaders of all time is Warren Buffett, chairman and CEO of Berkshire Hathaway. Buffett is revered for his exceptional investment prowess, integrity, and philanthropic efforts. He built Berkshire Hathaway into a conglomerate with a reputation for long-term value creation and prudent management. Buffett's down-to-earth demeanor, wisdom, and humility have earned him the admiration of investors worldwide. His steadfast adherence to fundamental investing principles and commitment to ethical business practices have solidified his status as a role model for aspiring entrepreneurs and investors alike.

C. Charisma

Charisma plays a significant role in being a great leader as it enables individuals to inspire, influence, and motivate others effectively. **Charismatic leaders possess a magnetic personality that attracts followers and commands** attention. Their confidence, enthusiasm, and persuasive communication skills make them compelling and inspiring figures. They have a strong vision for the future and the ability to articulate it in a way that resonates with others, igniting passion and enthusiasm among their team members. Their charisma creates a sense of excitement and energy, driving individuals to work towards shared goals with enthusiasm and dedication.

Charismatic leaders also have a natural ability to connect with people on an emotional level, building trust and rapport with their followers. They possess excellent interpersonal skills and empathy, making others feel valued and understood. They are adept at listening to their team members, providing encouragement and support, and fostering a sense of belonging and camaraderie within the organization. This ability to connect with others and create strong relationships contributes to their effectiveness as leaders.

Additionally, charisma enables leaders to influence and persuade others to support their vision and goals. **Charismatic leaders have a persuasive communication style and the ability to inspire confidence and enthusiasm in their ideas.** They are skilled at rallying people around a common cause, mobilizing support, and galvanizing action. Charismatic leaders have a powerful presence that captivates audiences and motivates individuals to follow their lead.

However, it's essential to recognize that charisma alone is not enough to make a great leader. While charisma can be an asset, effective leadership also requires integrity, humility, empathy, the ability to make sound decisions, and ultimately results. They must balance their natural charm with authenticity and ethical behavior to build trust and credibility with their followers. Ultimately, charisma is a powerful tool that can enhance a leader's effectiveness, but it must be coupled with other essential leadership qualities to achieve long-term success.

One renowned charismatic business leader is Richard Branson, founder of the Virgin Group. Branson's magnetic personality, adventurous spirit, and bold entrepreneurial endeavors have made him an icon in the business world. His charismatic leadership style is characterized by charm, optimism, and a willingness to take risks. Branson's ability to inspire and engage people from all walks of life has been instrumental in building the Virgin brand into a global empire encompassing diverse industries. His charisma extends beyond his public persona to his leadership approach, fostering innovation, creativity, and a sense of adventure among his team members.

D. Courage

Courage stands as an indispensable quality in effective leadership, serving as the bedrock upon which leaders navigate challenges, drive change, and inspire their teams to achieve greatness. **At its core, courage is the willingness to confront fear, uncertainty, and adversity head-on, even when the path forward may be daunting or fraught with obstacles.** Courageous leaders possess the resilience and fortitude to embrace change, recognizing that it often brings discomfort and uncertainty. In times of upheaval or transition, they remain steadfast, guiding their teams with confidence and composure, and making tough decisions when necessary. Whether it's restructuring teams, reallocating resources, or charting a new course for the organization, they lead with conviction, ensuring that their actions are aligned with the best interests of their teams and stakeholders.

Courage also empowers leaders to take calculated risks and seize opportunities for growth and innovation. Recognizing that progress often requires stepping outside of comfort zones and challenging the status quo, courageous leaders are unafraid to explore uncharted territory and push the boundaries of what's possible. They encourage creativity and experimentation, fostering a culture where team members feel empowered to voice their ideas and pursue bold initiatives. By fostering a culture of innovation and risk-taking, they propel their organizations forward, driving sustainable growth and competitive advantage in an ever-evolving marketplace.

Furthermore, courage enables leaders to speak truth to power, advocating for what they believe is right and standing up for the values and principles that define their leadership. **In the face of opposition or adversity, courageous leaders are unafraid to challenge the status quo, confront difficult issues, and champion necessary changes.** Whether it's addressing systemic injustices, advocating for diversity and inclusion, or confronting unethical practices, they lead by example, demonstrating integrity, authenticity, and moral courage in their actions and decisions.

Additionally, courage is essential for building trust and fostering meaningful connections within teams and organizations. By demonstrating vulnerability and authenticity, they create an environment where team members feel valued, heard, and respected. They encourage open communication, collaboration, and constructive feedback, fostering a culture of psychological safety where team members have the courage to express *their* ideas, share *their* concerns, and take calculated risks. By leading with courage and authenticity, leaders inspire trust and loyalty, building strong relationships that are essential for driving organizational success.

Ultimately, courage is a foundational element of effective leadership, enabling leaders to inspire confidence, drive change, and create lasting impact in their organizations and communities. By cultivating courage in their leadership approach, leaders can inspire others to overcome their fears, embrace challenges, and work together to achieve shared goals and aspirations.

Tim Cook, CEO of Apple Inc., epitomizes courage in leadership through his unwavering commitment to principles and willingness to take principled stands on important issues. His refusal to compromise on user privacy and encryption, even in the face of pressure from government agencies, demonstrates his dedication to protecting customer data. Additionally, Cook's advocacy for social and environmental responsibility, despite criticism from some shareholders, reflects his courage in standing up for what he believes is right. Through his leadership, Cook has not only steered Apple to unprecedented success but has also inspired others to prioritize ethics and social responsibility in business.

E. Positivity

Positivity is an indispensable trait in effective business leadership, offering a myriad of benefits that contribute to organizational success and employee well-being. One of the primary reasons positivity is important in leadership is its ability to cultivate a supportive and uplifting work environment. When leaders exude positivity, they create a culture where team members feel valued, appreciated, and motivated to give their best efforts. **This positive atmosphere fosters higher morale, increased engagement, and stronger bonds** among colleagues, ultimately leading to improved collaboration and teamwork.

Positivity also enables leaders to effectively navigate challenges and setbacks that inevitably arise in the business world. A positive outlook allows leaders to maintain resilience in the face of adversity, viewing obstacles as opportunities for growth and learning rather than insurmountable barriers. By approaching challenges with optimism and determination, they inspire confidence and motivation among their team members, encouraging them to persevere and find creative solutions to overcome obstacles.

Additionally, positivity in leadership contributes to a culture of trust and transparency within the organization. When they maintain a positive demeanor, they foster an environment where open communication, honesty, and mutual respect thrive. Team members are more likely to feel comfortable sharing their ideas, concerns, and feedback when they perceive their leaders as approachable and supportive. **This transparency facilitates stronger relationships between leaders and employees, leading to higher levels of trust, loyalty, and job satisfaction.**

Furthermore, positive leadership has a direct impact on employee well-being and mental health. Research has shown that a positive work environment can reduce stress, increase job satisfaction, and improve overall mental and emotional well-being among employees. **Positive leaders who prioritize employee happiness and well-being create a culture where individuals feel valued, supported, and fulfilled in their roles, leading to higher levels of job satisfaction, engagement, and retention.**

Positivity is a foundation of effective business leadership, offering numerous benefits for both leaders and their teams. By fostering a supportive and uplifting work environment, enabling leaders to navigate challenges with resilience and determination, promoting trust and transparency, and enhancing employee well-being, positivity plays a critical role in driving organizational success and fostering a culture of growth, innovation, and success. As such, cultivating positivity in leadership is essential for creating a thriving and sustainable business environment.

Ginni Rometty, the former CEO and Executive Chairman of IBM, is recognized as a positive business leader for her commitment to innovation, diversity and inclusion, corporate social responsibility, ethical leadership, and strategic vision. Under her leadership, IBM embraced transformative technologies, promoted diversity in the workplace, implemented sustainability initiatives, upheld ethical standards, and navigated the company through strategic transformations. Rometty's contributions to IBM and her advocacy for positive change in the tech industry underscore her impact as a leader who prioritizes values-driven leadership and making a meaningful difference in the world.

34

IV. Understanding Yourself as a Leader

Self-confidence is a foundational requirement for effective leadership, as it shapes a one's ability to inspire, motivate, and guide others. It is not merely about managing tasks and directing people; it involves building relationships, influencing behavior, and fostering a shared vision. When a leader is comfortable with themselves, they project confidence, authenticity, and integrity, which are essential qualities that inspire trust and respect in their followers.

Firstly, being comfortable with oneself enables someone to lead from a place of authenticity. Authentic leadership is grounded in self-awareness and genuine expression of one's values, beliefs, and principles. **A leader who is comfortable with themselves is more likely to lead authentically, staying true to their core identity and principles even in the face of challenges and adversity.** This authenticity fosters trust and confidence in the leader, as followers are more inclined to respect and follow someone who is genuine and true to themselves.

Moreover, it allows you to effectively manage your emotions and interpersonal dynamics. Emotional intelligence, or the ability to understand and manage your own emotions and those of others, is a critical leadership skill that is closely linked to self-awareness. This emotional resilience enables you to navigate interpersonal conflicts, communicate openly and transparently with your team members, and foster a positive and supportive work environment.

Leadership is inherently challenging and demanding, requiring leaders to navigate uncertainty, setbacks, and change. A leader who is comfortable with themselves is more emotionally resilient, able to handle stress and pressure with grace and composure, and better equipped to bounce back from setbacks and failures. They can stay focused and composed in the face of adversity, inspire confidence in their team members, and lead effectively through times of change and uncertainty.

It also enhances their ability to build strong and authentic relationships with their team members. **Trust is the foundation of effective leadership, and trust is built through genuine connection and rapport**. They are more likely to be open, transparent, and vulnerable with their team members, fostering trust and mutual respect. This trust creates a positive and supportive work environment where team members feel valued, empowered, and motivated to perform at their best.

Effective communication is a cornerstone of leadership, and it requires clarity, confidence, and conviction. **A leader who is comfortable with themselves is more likely to communicate with confidence and conviction, inspiring and motivating their team members to align with their vision and goals**. This clear and compelling communication fosters engagement, commitment, and buy-in from team members, driving organizational success and achieving positive outcomes.

Leaders are often relied on to effectively navigate complex and ambiguous situations, which often involves making tough decisions, taking risks, and confronting difficult and uncomfortable truths. A leader who is comfortable with themselves is more likely to embrace uncertainty and ambiguity, approaching challenges with curiosity, creativity, and open-mindedness. This adaptability enables them to navigate change and uncertainty with confidence and resilience, finding innovative solutions to complex problems and driving organizational success.

A. The Foundation of Leadership

At its core, self-awareness involves having a clear understanding of one's own emotions, thoughts, strengths, weaknesses, values, and motivations. This deep level of self-reflection allows leaders to recognize their impact on others, understand how their actions align with their values, and identify areas for growth and development.

One of the key reasons why self-awareness is foundational to leadership is its role in fostering authenticity. Authentic leadership is characterized by genuine self-awareness and integrity, with leaders leading from a place of sincerity and transparency. This authenticity fosters trust and credibility in the leader, as followers are more likely to respect and follow someone who is genuine and true to themselves.

Leaders who are self-aware are better equipped to recognize their own emotional triggers, regulate their emotions, and respond effectively to the emotions of others. This emotional resilience enables leaders to navigate interpersonal conflicts, communicate openly and transparently with their team members, and foster a positive and supportive work environment. This also comes in handy for those leaders who also interface with customers.

Self-awareness plays a vital role in enhancing a leader's ability to build strong and authentic relationships with their team members. Trust is the foundation of effective leadership, and trust is built through genuine connection, and it also takes time. This trust creates a positive and supportive work environment where team members feel valued, empowered, and motivated to perform at their best.

Being self-aware fosters resilience and adaptability within leaders, enabling them to navigate change, uncertainty, and complexity with confidence and composure. Leadership often involves making tough decisions, taking risks, and confronting difficult and uncomfortable truths. Leaders who possess a high degree of self-awareness are more likely to embrace uncertainty and ambiguity, approaching challenges with curiosity, creativity, and open-mindedness. This adaptability enables leaders to navigate change and uncertainty with confidence and resilience, finding innovative solutions to complex problems and driving organizational success.

B. Understand your Own Strengths and Weaknesses

Leaders who are vulnerable enough to uncover their own strengths and weaknesses knowledge can leverage their strengths to drive success while proactively addressing their weaknesses to mitigate potential challenges. This would allow you as a leader to embrace a culture of continuous improvement, authenticity, and adaptability within organizations.

Every leader possesses unique strengths, whether it be in strategic thinking, communication, decision-making, or relationship-building. By identifying and capitalizing on these strengths, leaders can play to their advantages, driving innovation, efficiency, and productivity within their teams. For example, someone with strong communication skills may excel at articulating a compelling vision, rallying team members around shared goals, and fostering a culture of collaboration and accountability. Leveraging strengths allows them to delegate tasks that align with their expertise, empowering team members to take ownership of their responsibilities and contribute to the organization's success.

No leader is without flaws, and acknowledging weaknesses is the first step towards improvement. **By accepting and addressing their limitations, leaders demonstrate humility, self-awareness, and a commitment to personal and professional growth.** Leaders can seek feedback from peers, mentors, and team members to identify areas where they may be deficient and develop strategies for improvement. For instance, a leader who struggles with delegation may prioritize building trust with their team members, clarifying expectations, and providing support and guidance as needed. Addressing weaknesses enables leaders to enhance their effectiveness, overcome obstacles, and adapt to changing circumstances within their organizations.

Moreover, understanding strengths and weaknesses informs decision-making processes, allowing someone to make more informed choices. Leaders who are self-aware recognize how their personal attributes may influence outcomes and consider the implications of their decisions on themselves, their teams, and their organizations. They know when to rely on their strengths to make decisive decisions and when to seek input or support in areas where they lack expertise. For example, a leader with strong analytical skills may excel at data-driven decision-making, while seeking input from subject matter experts to ensure comprehensive analysis and informed decision-making. By weighing the potential risks and benefits of different courses of action, leaders can make decisions that align with organizational goals, values, and priorities.

This doesn't just apply to the leader themselves, but this same analysis can be done for the team that you manage. Understanding how to leverage strengths and shore up weaknesses, will be critical to the collective success of your team.

By recognizing and leveraging strengths, leaders can maximize their impact within their organizations, while addressing weaknesses enables leaders to overcome obstacles and adapt to changing circumstances.

C. Leading with Integrity and Authenticity

Leaders with high levels of integrity demonstrate sincerity, transparency, and consistency in their words and actions, fostering an environment where trust flourishes. By embodying this trait, they cultivate strong relationships built on mutual respect and understanding, enabling them to navigate challenges and inspire confidence among team members. This trust forms the bedrock of effective leadership, allowing them to lead with conviction and purpose.

Moreover, integrity inspires engagement by fostering genuine connections between leaders and their teams. They recognize the individuality of each team member, demonstrating empathy, compassion, and appreciation for their unique contributions. This personal connection fosters a sense of belonging and camaraderie, motivating team members to fully invest their efforts towards achieving shared goals and objectives. When they lead authentically, they create an environment where team members feel valued, respected, and empowered to bring their whole selves to work.

Leaders are also able to clarify purpose by articulating a compelling vision grounded in values and beliefs. They can communicate this vision with honesty and transparency, inspiring team members to align their efforts towards a common cause. **By sharing their passion and enthusiasm for the organization's mission, authentic leaders ignite a sense of purpose and**

meaning among team members, driving collective action towards achieving organizational goals. This clarity of purpose guides decision-making, shapes priorities, and fuels the collective effort to realize the shared vision.

A leader with a high level of integrity encourages innovation by fostering a culture of openness, creativity, and experimentation. They embrace diversity of thought and welcome new ideas, recognizing that innovation thrives in an environment where all voices are heard and valued. By creating space for curiosity, exploration, and risk-taking, authentic leaders empower team members to challenge the status quo, explore new possibilities, and innovate new solutions to complex problems. This culture of innovation drives continuous improvement, fuels growth, and enhances the organization's competitive edge.

Moreover, this authenticity builds resilience by promoting vulnerability and adaptability in the face of adversity. When leaders acknowledge their own limitations, mistakes, and setbacks openly, they create a culture of psychological safety where team members feel comfortable taking risks and learning from failure. By demonstrating resilience and perseverance in the face of challenges, leaders inspire resilience in their teams, fostering a growth mindset and a willingness to embrace change and uncertainty.

Authenticity is also a powerful leadership attribute that enables leaders to lead with clarity of purpose, unwavering intent, and genuine connection. **Authentic leaders cultivate trust, inspire engagement, clarify purpose, encourage innovation, and promote resilience within their teams, driving organizational success and empowering individuals to realize their full potential.** By leading authentically, leaders create a culture of trust, collaboration, and innovation, where team members feel valued, respected, and motivated to contribute their best work towards achieving shared goals. Ultimately, authenticity is not just a leadership trait; it is a guiding principle that shapes the character and impact of leaders, inspiring greatness and driving positive change within organizations.

D. Leverage your Life Experiences

Leaders can leverage their personal and professional experiences to enhance their leadership effectiveness in several ways, drawing upon insights gained from both triumphs and setbacks to inform their decisions, inspire their teams, and drive organizational success.

They can use their personal experiences to cultivate empathy and understanding towards their team members. **By reflecting on their own challenges, triumphs, and growth journeys, leaders gain valuable perspective into the diverse experiences and perspectives of their team members.** This empathetic approach enables leaders to connect with their team on a deeper level, foster trust, and create a supportive work environment where team members feel valued, understood, and empowered to succeed.

They can also draw upon their professional experiences to inform their decision-making and problem-solving approaches. Leaders who have navigated complex challenges, overcome obstacles, and achieved success in their professional endeavors bring a wealth of practical knowledge and insights to their leadership roles. By reflecting on past experiences, leaders can identify patterns, lessons learned, and best practices that can be applied to current and future situations.

Everyone has a different mix of personal and professional experiences that they can use to relate, inspire, and motivate their teams. **Sharing stories of resilience, perseverance, and achievement from their own journeys can serve as powerful sources of inspiration for team members facing similar challenges.** By demonstrating vulnerability and authenticity, leaders create a culture where team members feel encouraged to embrace their own struggles, learn from failure, and strive for excellence. This shared sense of purpose and determination fosters camaraderie, teamwork, and collective success within the organization.

We can also use our diverse experiences to mentor and develop the next generation of leaders within their organizations. By sharing insights, providing guidance, and offering support to emerging leaders, experienced leaders can help cultivate a pipeline of talent and foster a culture of continuous learning and development. **Mentoring allows leaders to pass on valuable lessons learned from their own experiences, empowering others to navigate challenges, seize opportunities, and realize their full potential as leaders.**

Most leaders have experienced some level of change in their organizations that can be leveraged to enter the next change more confidently. Leaders who have witnessed firsthand the impact of evolving reporting structures, technology integrations, or even changing customer preferences are well-positioned to anticipate future trends and proactively adapt their organizations to stay ahead of the curve. By leveraging their insights and experience, leaders can champion innovation, foster a culture of experimentation, and drive strategic initiatives that position their organizations for long-term success in an ever-changing business landscape.

A true leader can use their personal and professional experiences to become more effective leaders by cultivating empathy, informing decision-making, inspiring, and motivating their teams, mentoring emerging leaders, driving organizational change and innovation.

E. Humor in Leadership

Using humor in leadership can be a powerful tool for fostering a positive and engaging work environment. When leaders incorporate humor into their interactions with team members, it can have several beneficial effects on both individuals and the team.

Humor helps to break down barriers and facilitate open communication. By injecting lightheartedness into discussions and meetings, leaders create a more relaxed atmosphere where team members feel comfortable expressing themselves and sharing ideas. This can lead to more productive brainstorming sessions and collaboration.

Humor can also build rapport and strengthen relationships within the team. **When leaders use humor appropriately, it humanizes them and makes them more relatable to their team members.** This can help to create a sense of camaraderie and trust, fostering a supportive and cohesive team dynamic.

Additionally, humor has the power to boost morale and alleviate stress. Laughter is said to be the best medicine and is a natural stress reliever. A good joke or witty remark can help team members unwind and recharge, particularly during challenging or high-pressure situations. By lightening the mood and injecting positivity into the workplace, leaders can help to create a more resilient and motivated team.

However, it's important for leaders to use humor judiciously and sparingly. **Not all situations are appropriate for humor, and leaders must be mindful of cultural sensitivities, individual preferences, and the context in which humor is used.** Humor should *never* be used at the expense of others or in a way that undermines professionalism or respect.

Humor can be a valuable tool for effective leadership, fostering open communication, building rapport, boosting morale, and stimulating creativity within teams. When used thoughtfully and respectfully, humor has the power to create a more positive and engaging work environment, leading to increased productivity, satisfaction, and success for both leaders and their teams.

44

V. Tailoring Your Leadership Approach

In the realm of business leadership, tailoring your leadership approach to your team is not just a beneficial practice, it's a strategic imperative. Here's what doing this will accomplish:

1. **Optimizing Performance**: Business leaders must ensure that their teams are performing at their peak to achieve organizational objectives. By understanding the diverse strengths, preferences, and work styles of team members, leaders can tailor their approach to maximize individual and collective performance. For example, some team members may thrive on autonomy and independence, while others may prefer or need more guidance and direction. By recognizing these differences and adjusting their leadership style accordingly, leaders can optimize team performance and drive better results.

2. **Fostering Innovation**: In today's competitive business landscape, innovation is key to staying ahead of the curve. Effective leadership involves creating an environment where creativity and innovation can flourish. By tailoring their leadership approach to support the unique needs and preferences of their team members, leaders can foster a culture of innovation where individuals feel empowered to share ideas, take risks, and explore new approaches. This not only boosts creativity and problem-solving but also drives business growth and competitiveness.

3. **Building High-Performing Teams**: High-performing teams are the backbone of successful businesses. However, building and maintaining such teams requires more than just assembling a group of talented individuals. It requires strong leadership that recognizes and leverages the diverse strengths and abilities of team members. By tailoring their leadership approach to foster collaboration, trust, and accountability, leaders can build high-performing teams that can achieve extraordinary results. Within every high performing team there is usually a mix of productivity. Let the productive employees open their wings and dedicate time to the underperforming employees to lift them up to standard.

4. **Driving Employee Engagement and Retention**: Employee engagement and retention are critical concerns for businesses looking to attract and retain top talent. Research has consistently shown that employees are more engaged and committed when they feel valued, supported, and understood by their leaders. By tailoring their leadership approach to meet the needs and preferences of their team members, leaders can create a positive work environment where employees feel motivated, engaged, and invested in the success of the organization. This, in turn, leads to higher levels of employee satisfaction, lower turnover rates, and greater overall success for the business.

5. **Adapting to Market Dynamics**: The business landscape is constantly evolving, with new challenges and opportunities emerging regularly. Effective leaders must be able to adapt to these changing dynamics quickly and effectively. By tailoring their leadership approach to fit the specific circumstances and challenges facing their team, leaders can navigate uncertainties, capitalize on opportunities, and drive sustainable growth for the business.

Tailoring your leadership approach to your team is essential for optimizing performance, fostering innovation, building high-performing teams, driving employee engagement and retention, and adapting to market dynamics.

By understanding and accommodating the unique needs and preferences of their team members, business leaders can create a positive and supportive work environment where individuals thrive, businesses succeed, and goals are achieved.

A. Recognizing Individual Differences Amongst Your Team

Recognizing the individual differences amongst your team is critical for effective leadership and team dynamics. In today's diverse workplace, understanding and appreciating the unique attributes of each team member can significantly impact overall performance, collaboration, and morale. Here's why recognizing individual differences is essential:

1. **Effective Communication:** Communication lies at the heart of successful leadership. By recognizing individual differences, leaders can tailor their communication styles to suit the preferences and needs of each team member. Some individuals may prefer direct and concise communication, while others may appreciate a more detailed and nuanced approach. By understanding these preferences, leaders can ensure that their messages are clear, concise, and well-received, leading to better understanding and collaboration within the team.

2. **Maximizing Strengths:** Each team member brings a unique set of skills, talents, and perspectives to the table. By recognizing and leveraging these individual strengths, leaders can enhance team performance and productivity. For example, a team member with strong analytical skills may excel at problem-solving tasks, while another with exceptional interpersonal skills may thrive in client-facing roles. By harnessing these strengths, leaders can allocate tasks and responsibilities more effectively, leading to a more balanced and high-performing team.

3. **Supporting Development:** Every team member has their own career aspirations, goals, and areas for development. Recognizing

individual differences allows leaders to provide personalized support and guidance to help team members reach their full potential. This may involve offering tailored training programs, mentorship opportunities, or challenging assignments that align with everyone's career aspirations and development goals. By investing in the growth and development of their team members, leaders foster a culture of continuous learning and strengthen employee engagement and retention.

4. **Building Trust and Rapport:** Trust is a fundamental component of effective leadership and team dynamics. By recognizing and respecting individual differences, leaders demonstrate empathy, understanding, and appreciation for each team member's unique contributions and perspectives. When team members feel valued and respected, they are more likely to trust their leader and feel a sense of loyalty and commitment to the team and organization. This fosters stronger relationships, enhances collaboration, and promotes a positive and supportive work environment.

5. **Promoting Diversity and Inclusion:** Diversity and inclusion are essential principles in today's workplace. Recognizing and embracing individual differences is crucial for creating a culture of diversity and inclusion where all team members feel valued, respected, and empowered to contribute their unique perspectives and insights. By promoting diversity and inclusion, leaders foster innovation and creativity and create a more welcoming and inclusive work environment that attracts and retains top talent from diverse backgrounds.

6. **Resolving Conflicts:** Conflicts and disagreements are inevitable in any team environment. However, recognizing individual differences can help leaders effectively address and resolve conflicts in a constructive manner. By understanding each team member's unique communication style, preferences, and motivations, leaders can facilitate open and honest dialogue, promote mutual understanding, and find solutions that are acceptable to all parties involved. This strengthens relationships

within the team and fosters a culture of trust, respect, and collaboration.

7. **Driving Engagement and Satisfaction:** Employee engagement and satisfaction are critical drivers of organizational success. Recognizing individual differences and providing personalized support and recognition can significantly impact employee engagement and satisfaction levels. When team members feel valued, respected, and appreciated for their unique contributions, they are more likely to feel motivated, engaged, and committed to their work and the organization as a whole. This leads to higher levels of productivity, creativity, and overall job satisfaction, ultimately driving better business outcomes.

Recognizing individual differences amongst your team is essential for effective leadership, collaboration, and team performance. By tailoring communication, maximizing strengths, supporting development, building trust and rapport, promoting diversity and inclusion, resolving conflicts, and driving engagement and satisfaction, leaders can create a positive and inclusive work environment where all team members can thrive and contribute to the organization's success.

B. Adapting Your Leadership Style to Different Situations

Adapting your leadership style to different situations and challenges is paramount in cultivating a successful and resilient team. Leaders must possess the ability to flexibly navigate various scenarios, addressing each with an approach tailored to its unique demands. This adaptability is not just a skill but a mindset, one that allows leaders to empower their teams, build strong relationships, and optimize performance in diverse contexts.

Flexibility lies at the core of adaptive leadership. Different situations call for different strategies, and leaders who can pivot seamlessly between styles are better equipped to guide their teams through various challenges. For instance, in a crisis scenario where urgent decisions need to be made, a directive leadership style may be necessary to provide clarity and decisiveness.

Conversely, in a brainstorming session aimed at fostering creativity and innovation, a more democratic approach that encourages open dialogue and participation may be more effective. **By understanding the nuances of each situation and adapting their leadership style accordingly, leaders can create an environment conducive to success.**

Furthermore, adaptability empowers team members to take ownership of their work and contribute meaningfully to the team's objectives. When leaders demonstrate flexibility and trust in their team's capabilities, it fosters a sense of autonomy and accountability among team members. **This empowerment not only boosts morale but also encourages innovation and creativity as team members feel empowered to explore new ideas and approaches without fear of judgment.**

Adaptability is closely linked to resilience. In today's volatile business environment, teams must be able to adapt quickly to changing circumstances and overcome obstacles with agility. Leaders who can adapt their approach to address challenges effectively help their teams build resilience and bounce back from setbacks stronger than before. By fostering a culture of adaptability and resilience, leaders equip their teams with the mindset and tools needed to navigate uncertainty and thrive in the face of adversity.

Relationship building is another crucial aspect of adaptive leadership. Recognizing and respecting individual differences among team members is essential for building strong relationships based on trust and mutual respect. By adapting their leadership style to accommodate diverse personalities and preferences, leaders demonstrate their commitment to understanding and supporting each team member's unique needs and contributions. This fosters a sense of belonging and camaraderie within the team, leading to stronger collaboration and higher levels of engagement. **By building strong relationships with team members, leaders can better understand their strengths, weaknesses, and motivations, enabling them to tailor their leadership approach to maximize individual and collective performance.**

Optimizing performance requires leaders to adapt their leadership style to meet the specific demands of each situation. In high-pressure environments where quick decisions are needed, a more directive leadership style may be necessary to provide clear direction and guidance. On the other hand, in situations that require creativity and collaboration, a more participative approach that encourages input from team members may be more effective.

Cultural sensitivity is also critical in adaptive leadership. In today's globalized world, teams often consist of members from diverse cultural backgrounds. Leaders who can adapt their leadership style to accommodate cultural differences demonstrate respect and inclusivity, fostering a more harmonious and collaborative team environment. By being mindful of cultural nuances and adapting their communication and leadership approach accordingly, leaders can build stronger relationships and enhance team cohesion.

Adaptive leadership is essential for cultivating a successful and resilient team in today's complex and dynamic business environment. By being flexible, empowering, and resilient, leaders can navigate various challenges and opportunities effectively, optimizing performance and driving success. Through relationship building, performance optimization, cultural sensitivity, and resilience, adaptive leaders can create a positive and inclusive team environment where all members can thrive and contribute to the organization's success.

VI.   Building High-Performing Teams

A true leader possesses the ability to create a high-performing team by fostering an environment of trust, collaboration, and accountability. Firstly, they establish clear goals and expectations, ensuring that every team member understands their role and responsibilities within the larger context of the team's objectives. By providing clarity and direction, the leader sets the stage for alignment and focus, enabling team members to work towards common goals with a shared sense of purpose. Additionally, a good leader cultivates a culture of open communication and feedback, encouraging team members to share ideas, voice concerns, and provide constructive input. This open dialogue promotes transparency and collaboration, fostering a sense of ownership and buy-in among team members.

The team leader creates a high-performing team by establishing clear goals and expectations, fostering open communication and collaboration, leading by example, and investing in the development of their team members. Through these efforts, the leader builds a cohesive and motivated team that consistently delivers exceptional results.

A. Inspiring Others to Follow

A leader who creates a compelling vision has the power to inspire others to follow them by tapping into the aspirations, values, and emotions of their team members. Firstly, a visionary leader articulates a clear and compelling vision that resonates with the aspirations and values of their team members. By painting a vivid picture of a desirable outcome, the leader captures the imagination and ignites the passion of their team, inspiring them to align their efforts towards achieving the shared vision.

They also communicate their vision with enthusiasm, conviction, and authenticity, evoking a sense of purpose and excitement among team members. Through passionate storytelling and persuasive communication, the leader creates an emotional connection with their audience, inspiring them to believe in the vision and commit to its realization. They don't just talk the talk, but they walk the walk. They lead by example, demonstrating their commitment to the vision through *their* actions and behavior. By embodying the values and principles of the vision in their own leadership approach, the leader inspires trust, respect, and confidence in their followers, motivating them to emulate the leader's example and fully invest themselves in the pursuit of the vision.

A visionary leader empowers their team members to contribute their ideas, insights, and talents towards shaping and executing the vision. **By fostering a culture of collaboration, innovation, and inclusivity, the leader taps into the collective wisdom and creativity of their team, harnessing the full potential of every individual towards achieving the shared vision.** A leader who creates a compelling vision, inspires others to follow them by articulating a clear and compelling vision, communicating with enthusiasm and authenticity, leading by example, and empowering their team members to contribute towards the realization of the vision. Through these efforts, the leader ignites the passion and commitment of their followers, galvanizing them to work together towards a common purpose and achieve extraordinary results.

One of the most famous inspirational leaders of all time is Mahatma Gandhi. He is revered for his unwavering commitment to nonviolent resistance and his role in India's struggle for independence from British rule. Gandhi's leadership was characterized by his principles of truth, nonviolence, and self-sacrifice, which inspired millions around the world to embrace the ideals of peace, justice, and equality. His ability to mobilize mass movements through peaceful protest and civil disobedience demonstrated the transformative power of moral leadership. Gandhi's legacy continues to inspire generations of leaders to advocate for social change, human rights, and the pursuit of justice through peaceful means.

B. Team Roles and Group Dynamics

Understanding team roles and group dynamics is crucial for a leader to drive more results by effectively leveraging the strengths of individual team members, fostering collaboration, and optimizing team performance. **By comprehending the unique skills, strengths, and expertise of each team member, a leader can strategically assign tasks and responsibilities, ensuring that they align with the capabilities and preferences of everyone.** This targeted delegation maximizes efficiency and productivity within the team, as members are empowered to contribute to areas where they excel. Additionally, understanding group dynamics enables a leader to identify potential conflicts, communication barriers, or performance gaps within the team. By recognizing these dynamics, the leader can proactively address issues, facilitate constructive dialogue, and foster a culture of open communication and trust. This proactive approach fosters a supportive environment where team members feel valued, heard, and motivated to collaborate towards common goals.

Furthermore, understanding team roles and dynamics facilitates collaboration and synergy among team members. By encouraging diverse perspectives, fostering a culture of mutual respect, and creating opportunities for teamwork and knowledge-sharing, the leader can harness the collective intelligence and creativity of the team to drive innovation and problem-solving. When team members feel empowered to contribute their ideas and insights, they become more invested in the success of the team, leading to increased engagement and commitment. **By recognizing and appreciating the unique contributions of each team member, the leader fosters a sense of belonging and camaraderie within the team.** This sense of unity motivates team members to perform at their best and support one another in achieving shared goals.

By optimizing team performance through effective leadership, a leader can achieve better results. By setting clear expectations, providing feedback and guidance, and offering support and resources as needed, the leader empowers team members to reach their full potential. Additionally, **the leader plays a critical role in removing obstacles, resolving conflicts, and facilitating decision-making, enabling the team to stay focused and productive.** When team members feel supported and valued by their leader, they are more likely to go above and beyond to deliver exceptional results.

Fully understanding team roles and group dynamics is essential for a leader to drive more results by strategically assigning tasks, addressing conflicts, fostering collaboration, and optimizing team performance. **A collaborative leader can harness the collective potential of the team and achieve extraordinary results.** By recognizing and appreciating the unique contributions of each team member and fostering a culture of open communication and trust, the leader creates a supportive environment where team members feel empowered to collaborate, innovate, and excel.

C. The Art of Listening

Effective communication, particularly through the art of listening, is essential for a leader to create a high-performing team that consistently exceeds results. In today's dynamic and fast-paced work environment, effective communication serves as the cornerstone for building trust, fostering collaboration, and driving innovation within teams. By prioritizing active listening, soliciting feedback, and providing constructive input, leaders can cultivate a culture of openness, accountability, and continuous improvement that empowers team members to achieve extraordinary results.

Active listening is a foundational aspect of effective communication that enables leaders to truly understand the perspectives, concerns, and aspirations of their team members. When leaders actively listen, they demonstrate respect, empathy, and attentiveness, creating a supportive environment where team members feel valued and understood. Active listening involves not only hearing what is being said but also paying attention to nonverbal cues, such as body language and tone of voice, which provide valuable insights into the underlying emotions and motivations of the speaker. By actively engaging in the conversation, asking clarifying questions, and paraphrasing key points, leaders can demonstrate their commitment to understanding and addressing the needs of their team members. They also foster trust and rapport between leaders and team members, laying the foundation for open and honest communication that drives collaboration and innovation. **Fight the urge to multitask during meetings with your team when your attention and participation can have a positive effect on the outcome of the meeting.**

Soliciting feedback from team members is another critical component of effective communication that empowers leaders to continuously improve and evolve. **By actively seeking input from team members, leaders demonstrate humility, openness, and a willingness to learn from others.** Feedback provides valuable information about what is working well and areas for improvement, enabling leaders to identify opportunities for growth, address challenges, and optimize team performance.

Moreover, involving team members in the decision-making process and incorporating their feedback into strategic initiatives fosters a sense of ownership and commitment, leading to greater engagement and buy-in from the team.

Additionally, providing constructive feedback to team members is essential for helping them grow and develop professionally. By offering specific, timely, and actionable feedback, leaders empower team members to identify areas for improvement, build on their strengths, and achieve their full potential. Constructive feedback also helps clarify expectations, align goals, and facilitate performance improvement, leading to greater accountability and results. **You may not always like what you are hearing when someone is giving you feedback. Try not to take it personally and be offended. It takes courage to give feedback, but also to take it.**

By aligning goals and objectives with the organization's mission and values, leaders create a sense of meaning and significance that resonates with team members on a personal level. Effective communication involves celebrating the achievements and contributions of team members, reinforcing positive behaviors, and fostering a culture of appreciation and recognition within the team. By acknowledging the hard work and dedication of team members, leaders boost morale, enhance job satisfaction, and cultivate a sense of pride and belonging that inspires loyalty and commitment.

D. Fostering a Culture of Collaboration and Innovation

Fostering a culture of collaboration and innovation is instrumental in helping a leader create a strong team that is cohesive, motivated, and adaptable to change. **By prioritizing innovation, leaders empower team members to**

leverage their diverse perspectives, talents, and experiences to achieve common goals and drive organizational success.

Firstly, a culture of collaboration encourages open communication, trust, and mutual respect among team members. When leaders foster an environment where individuals feel valued and supported, team members are more likely to collaborate effectively, share ideas, and work towards common objectives. Collaboration enables team members to leverage each other's strengths, address weaknesses, and fill gaps in knowledge or expertise, leading to more robust solutions and better outcomes. **Collaboration promotes a sense of ownership and accountability, as team members feel personally invested in the success of the team and are motivated to contribute their best work.**

Furthermore, a culture of innovation encourages creativity, experimentation, and risk-taking within the team. When leaders create an environment where new ideas are welcomed and celebrated, team members are inspired to think outside the box, challenge the status quo, and explore new possibilities. Innovation enables teams to adapt to changing market conditions, identify emerging opportunities, and solve complex problems in innovative ways. Fostering a culture of innovation demonstrates to team members that their contributions are valued and that their ideas have the potential to make a real impact, increasing motivation, engagement, and job satisfaction.

Additionally, collaboration and innovation go hand in hand, as diverse perspectives and ideas often lead to breakthrough innovations and transformative solutions. When leaders encourage cross-functional collaboration and create opportunities for interdisciplinary teamwork, they enable team members to leverage their unique skills and perspectives to tackle complex challenges from multiple angles. This multidisciplinary approach fosters creativity, sparks innovation, and drives continuous improvement within the team.

Fostering a culture of collaboration and innovation helps leaders build resilience and adaptability within their teams. By promoting collaboration and innovation, leaders equip their teams with the skills, mindset, and tools needed to navigate uncertainty and embrace change. It enables teams to quickly mobilize resources, share knowledge, and coordinate efforts in response to challenges or opportunities, while innovation enables teams to develop creative solutions and pivot strategies in real-time.

E. Delicate Balance of Management vs Micromanagement

Finding the delicate balance between effective management and micromanagement is crucial for a leader who aims to drive results while maintaining a positive work environment and fostering growth among team members. **Management involves providing guidance, direction, and support to ensure that tasks are completed efficiently and effectively, while micromanagement involves excessive oversight and control over every detail of the work process, often stifling creativity, autonomy, and morale within the team.**

Effective management entails setting clear expectations, providing necessary resources and support, and holding team members accountable for their performance. It involves delegating tasks and responsibilities based on everyone's strengths and capabilities, while providing sufficient autonomy and empowerment for team members to execute their work independently. **A manager who practices effective management focuses on outcomes and results, rather than dictating how every task should be completed.** They trust their team members to deliver results and provide guidance and support as needed, fostering a sense of ownership and accountability within the team.

On the other hand, micromanagement occurs when a leader excessively monitors and controls the work of their team members, often out of a fear of losing control or a lack of trust in their abilities. Micromanagers tend to be overly involved in every aspect of the work process, constantly checking in, making changes, and second-guessing decisions made by their team members. This can lead to decreased morale, autonomy, and motivation among team members, as well as increased stress and burnout.

For a leader driving towards results, finding the balance between management and micromanagement is essential. **While it's important to provide guidance, support, and oversight to ensure that tasks are completed effectively, it's equally important to trust and empower team members to take ownership of their work and make decisions autonomously.** Leaders should focus on setting clear expectations, providing necessary resources and support, and holding team members accountable for their performance, while allowing them the freedom to work in their own way and leverage their unique strengths and expertise.

To strike this delicate balance, leaders can adopt several strategies:

1. **Set clear expectations:** Clearly communicate goals, objectives, and performance standards to ensure that team members understand what is expected of them and how their work contributes to the overall goals of the team and organization.

2. **Provide support and resources**: Ensure that team members have the necessary tools, resources, and training to successfully execute their work. Offer guidance, feedback, and coaching to help them overcome challenges and develop their skills.

3. **Delegate tasks appropriately**: Delegate tasks and responsibilities based on each team member's strengths, skills, and expertise. Trust team members to take ownership of their work and make decisions independently.

4. **Foster open communication**: Create a culture of open communication where team members feel comfortable sharing ideas, asking questions, and providing feedback. Encourage collaboration and knowledge-sharing to promote innovation and continuous improvement.

5. **Trust and empower team members**: Trust team members to execute their work effectively and make decisions autonomously. Avoid the temptation to micromanage and instead focus on supporting and empowering team members to achieve their goals.

6. **Provide opportunities for growth**: Encourage professional development and growth opportunities for team members to help

them expand their skills, knowledge, and capabilities. Recognize and reward their achievements and contributions to foster a sense of motivation and engagement.

By striking the right balance between management and micromanagement, leaders can drive results while maintaining a positive work environment, fostering growth among team members, and achieving long-term success for the organization.

F. Get Friendly, But Not Too Friendly

It's important for a leader to establish a friendly and supportive relationship with their team members, but it's equally important to maintain appropriate professional boundaries to avoid blurring the lines between personal and professional relationships. Building rapport and fostering a positive working relationship with team members helps create a supportive and inclusive work environment where individuals feel valued, respected, and motivated to perform at their best. Friendly interactions can also promote trust, communication, and collaboration within the team, leading to increased morale and productivity.

However, it's essential for leaders to be mindful of maintaining professional boundaries to avoid potential pitfalls that can arise from becoming too friendly with their team members. **When leaders become overly familiar or personal with their team, it can lead to perceptions of favoritism, bias, or lack of objectivity in decision-making.** Additionally, overly friendly relationships can undermine the leader's authority and credibility, making it difficult to enforce policies, address performance issues, or make tough decisions when necessary.

Furthermore, blurring the lines between personal and professional relationships can create confusion and discomfort among team members, particularly if they feel pressured to socialize outside of work or share personal information with their leader. This can lead to feelings of unease, resentment, or even harassment in extreme cases, which can have a detrimental impact on team dynamics and morale.

Therefore, while it's important for leaders to be approachable, supportive, and empathetic towards their team members, it's equally important to maintain a level of professionalism and objectivity in their interactions. Leaders should strive to create a balance between being friendly and maintaining appropriate boundaries, ensuring that their actions and behaviors align with the expectations of their role as a leader. By striking this balance, leaders can foster positive relationships with their team members while upholding their authority, credibility, and effectiveness as leaders.

G. Strength of the Leader is Dependent on the Strength of the Team

A business leader's effectiveness and success are intimately intertwined with the strength, cohesion, and capabilities of their team. While the leader sets the strategic direction and provides guidance, it is the collective effort and collaboration of the team members that translate vision into action and drive organizational success. The interdependence between leader and team underscores the significance of cultivating a supportive, engaged, and high-performing team culture.

One of the primary reasons why a business leader is only as strong as their team lies in the execution of the organizational vision and strategy. A leader may possess visionary insights and strategic acumen, but without a capable and motivated team to execute on those strategies, organizational goals remain unattainable. It is the team members who bring the leader's vision to life through their collective efforts, skills, and dedication. By leveraging the diverse talents and expertise of the team, leaders can overcome challenges, seize opportunities, and achieve sustainable growth.

A strong team fosters a collaborative culture where open communication, trust, and mutual respect thrive. Collaboration is essential for tackling complex problems, driving innovation, and fostering creativity within the organization. **When team members collaborate effectively, they bring diverse perspectives and ideas to the table, leading to more robust solutions and better outcomes.** By encouraging teamwork and collaboration, leaders create an environment where individuals feel valued, supported, and empowered to contribute their best work.

A strong team is characterized by its adaptability and resilience in the face of change and uncertainty. In today's fast-paced business environment, organizations must be agile and responsive to emerging trends and market dynamics. **A resilient team can quickly adapt to changing circumstances, pivot strategies, and overcome obstacles with determination and resourcefulness.** By fostering a culture of adaptability and resilience, leaders equip their teams to navigate challenges and seize opportunities effectively, ensuring the organization's continued success and relevance.

Another critical aspect of a strong team is employee engagement and retention. Engaged employees are more committed, motivated, and productive, leading to improved performance and business outcomes. A strong team culture, characterized by a sense of purpose, belonging, and shared values, fosters high levels of employee engagement. When team members feel valued, respected, and supported by their leaders and peers, they are more likely to remain with the organization and contribute their talents and ideas towards achieving its goals.

A leader's effectiveness is measured not only by their own achievements but also by the development and success of their team members. A strong leader invests in the growth and development of their team, providing opportunities for learning, skill-building, and career advancement. By empowering team members to reach their full potential, leaders cultivate a pipeline of talent and ensure the organization's long-term success and sustainability.

H. The Challenge of Managing Remote Teams

The rise of remote work has reshaped the way teams collaborate and operate, presenting both opportunities and challenges for leaders. With advancements in technology enabling seamless communication and collaboration across distances, remote work has become increasingly common, offering flexibility and autonomy for employees while also requiring leaders to adapt their management approach. Effective leaders must navigate the unique dynamics of remote teams, fostering a sense of connection, engagement, and accountability among team members.

1. **Building Trust and Communication**: In a remote work environment or a leader with a very large territory, building trust and maintaining open lines of communication are paramount. Leaders must establish clear channels for communication, leveraging tools such as video conferencing, instant messaging, and project management platforms to keep teams connected and informed. Regular check-ins and virtual team meetings provide opportunities for alignment, feedback, and relationship-building, helping to foster a sense of belonging and cohesion among remote team members.

2. **Setting Clear Expectations and Goals**: Remote work requires clarity and alignment around expectations and goals. Leaders must communicate clear objectives, priorities, and deadlines, ensuring that remote team members understand their roles and responsibilities. Setting SMART (Specific, Measurable, Achievable, Relevant, Time-bound) goals provides a framework for accountability and performance management, enabling remote teams to stay focused and productive.

3. **Promoting Collaboration and Team Building**: Despite physical distance, remote teams can foster collaboration and camaraderie through virtual team-building activities, collaborative projects, and informal social interactions. Leaders can facilitate virtual brainstorming sessions, collaborative document editing, and online team games to foster creativity and engagement. Building a sense of community and connection among remote team members helps to strengthen relationships and foster a positive team culture.

4. **Providing Support and Resources**: Remote work can be isolating and challenging, particularly for team members who may struggle with technology or communication barriers. Leaders must provide ongoing support and resources to help remote team members overcome

obstacles and thrive in their roles. This may include access to training and development opportunities, technical support, and mental health resources. By demonstrating empathy and understanding, leaders can create a supportive environment where remote team members feel valued and empowered to succeed.

5. **Embracing Flexibility and Adaptability**: Remote work requires leaders to embrace flexibility and adaptability, accommodating the diverse needs and preferences of remote team members. Leaders must be open to alternative work schedules, time zones, and communication styles, recognizing that what works for one team member may not work for another. Flexibility allows remote teams to maintain work-life balance and well-being while also achieving business objectives.

Managing a remote team requires a unique set of skills and approaches, characterized by effective communication, trust-building, goal setting, collaboration, and flexibility. By embracing the opportunities of remote work and addressing its challenges, leaders can empower remote teams to achieve their full potential, drive innovation, and deliver exceptional results.

VII. Leading Through Change, Uncertainty and Transformation

Leadership through change, uncertainty, and transformation is paramount in today's dynamic business landscape. Leaders who possess this ability are instrumental in guiding their teams through turbulent times, instilling confidence, and stability amidst uncertainty. By effectively navigating change, leaders inspire trust and foster a culture of adaptability within their organizations. They communicate the rationale behind change initiatives, address concerns empathetically, and mobilize their teams to embrace transformational opportunities.

Leading through change requires resilience – the ability to bounce back from setbacks and adversity. Resilient leaders model this resilience for their teams, demonstrating optimism, perseverance, and adaptability in the face of challenges. **They create a culture of psychological safety where team members feel empowered to challenge the status quo, innovate, and drive continuous improvement.**

Ultimately, leaders who excel in leading through change and uncertainty drive organizational agility, innovation, and long-term success in today's ever-evolving business landscape.

A. The Challenges of Leading in Turbulent Times

Leading in turbulent times presents leaders with a myriad of challenges that demand resilience, adaptability, and strategic acumen. Chief among these challenges is the general uncertainty that characterizes turbulent periods, encompassing economic conditions, external market volatility, and internal company policy changes. Leaders must navigate this uncertainty while formulating and executing strategies to steer their organizations through unpredictable terrain. **The rapid pace of change during turbulent times can be overwhelming, requiring leaders to make swift decisions and adjust course in response to evolving circumstances.**

Turbulent times also exert significant strain on employee well-being, as heightened stress and anxiety become prevalent. **Leaders must prioritize the mental health and resilience of their teams, offering support, flexibility, and resources to help employees navigate challenging times.**

Supply chain disruptions, financial constraints, cost of capital, high inflation and crisis situations further compound the challenges faced by leaders, demanding effective crisis management, stakeholder engagement, and long-term planning. Amidst these obstacles, maintaining focus, morale, and a sense of purpose within the organization becomes paramount. Leaders must inspire confidence, provide clear direction, and reinforce organizational values to keep teams motivated and engaged amid uncertainty.

In essence, leading in turbulent times demands a multifaceted approach, requiring leaders to exhibit agility, empathy, and strategic foresight as they navigate uncharted waters and steer their organizations toward stability and resilience.

The intrusive uncertainty that characterizes turbulent times poses one of the most significant challenges for leaders. Turbulent changes are often unpredictable, making it difficult for leaders to plan and make informed financial decisions. Leaders must navigate this uncertainty with confidence and clarity, inspiring trust, and stability within their teams. **By providing a steady hand and ear during turbulent times, leaders help alleviate anxiety and maintain focus on the organization's goals.**

Another challenge of leading in turbulent times is the rapid pace of change. Circumstances can evolve rapidly, requiring leaders to adapt quickly and make decisions in real-time. Whether it's adjusting business strategies, reallocating resources, or responding to emerging challenges, leaders must remain agile and flexible to effectively navigate change and uncertainty.

The transition to remote work, prompted by global events, introduces additional complexities for leaders. Managing remote teams effectively, fostering communication, and sustaining productivity in virtual environments require new skills and strategies. **Leaders must find innovative ways to engage and motivate their teams, despite physical distance and technological barriers.**

Employee well-being is another critical consideration during turbulent times. Heightened stress, anxiety, and burnout can take a toll on team members' mental health and performance. Leaders must prioritize the well-being of their teams, offering support, flexibility, and resources to help employees cope with stress and uncertainty.

Crisis situations, such as natural disasters, public health emergencies, or cybersecurity breaches, can also test leaders' abilities to manage uncertainty and adversity. Effective crisis management requires leaders to remain calm under pressure, communicate transparently with stakeholders, and make timely decisions to mitigate risks and ensure business continuity.

Despite these challenges, maintaining focus, morale, and a sense of purpose within the organization is essential. Leaders must inspire confidence, provide clear direction, and reinforce organizational values to keep teams motivated and engaged amid uncertainty. By fostering a positive and resilient culture, leaders can help their organizations weather the storm and emerge stronger on the other side.

B. Strategies for Leading Change Effectively & Building Resilience

Leading change effectively and building resilience in your team requires strategic planning and proactive management. Here are five strategies to achieve this:

1. **Communicate Transparently**: Transparent communication is vital for leading change effectively. Keep your team informed about the reasons for change, its potential impact, and the desired outcomes. Address concerns and questions openly, fostering a sense of trust and understanding. Regular updates and opportunities for feedback ensure that team members feel involved and engaged throughout the change process.

2. **Empower and Involve Employees**: Empower your team members to be active participants in the change process. Encourage them to contribute ideas, insights, and solutions, fostering a sense of ownership and commitment. Involving employees in decision-making and problem-solving builds resilience by empowering them to adapt and contribute to the success of the change initiative.

3. **Provide Support and Resources**: Change can be challenging, so it's essential to provide support and resources to help your team navigate the transition effectively. Offer training, coaching, and mentoring to develop new skills and capabilities needed to thrive in the changing environment. Provide access to information, tools, and guidance to facilitate the change process and alleviate concerns.

4. **Lead by Example**: As a leader, your actions speak louder than words. Model the behaviors and attitudes you want to see in your team members, demonstrating resilience, adaptability, and positivity in the face of change. Show empathy and understanding towards team members' concerns and challenges, while also maintaining a focus on the vision and goals of the change initiative. Your leadership sets the tone for how your team responds to change and builds resilience.

5. **Celebrate Progress and Successes**: Recognize and celebrate milestones, achievements, and successes along the way. Acknowledge the efforts and contributions of team members, highlighting the progress made towards the desired outcomes. Celebrating small wins boosts morale, motivation, and confidence, reinforcing the resilience of your team and sustaining momentum throughout the change journey.

By implementing these strategies, you can lead change effectively and build resilience in your team, enabling them to adapt, thrive, and succeed in the face of uncertainty and challenges. **Transparent communication,** empowerment, support, leading by example, and celebrating progress are key elements of a comprehensive approach to leading change and fostering resilience within your team.

C. Conflict Resolution

Conflict resolution is indispensable for business leaders, serving as a linchpin for managing both internal and external conflicts within organizations.

Internally, conflict resolution is paramount for navigating the intricate web of interpersonal dynamics and team interactions. **Within teams and departments, conflicts may arise due to differences in personality, work styles, or competing priorities.** In such cases, leaders must adeptly address conflicts to prevent them from festering and negatively impacting team morale and productivity. By fostering open communication, active listening, and collaboration, leaders can guide team members toward resolution, ensuring that conflicts are resolved constructively and that relationships are maintained and strengthened.

Externally, conflict resolution is equally vital for managing relationships with external stakeholders, including clients, partners, and suppliers. Disputes may arise over contractual obligations, disagreements in project scope, or diverging interests. Here, leaders must navigate conflicts with tact and diplomacy, seeking win-win solutions that preserve relationships and uphold the organization's reputation. **By engaging in effective negotiation, visualization, and conflict resolution techniques, leaders can mitigate potential risks, protect the organization's interests, and foster positive long-term relationships with external stakeholders.**

In both internal and external contexts, conflict resolution contributes to the cultivation of a positive organizational culture characterized by trust, collaboration, and resilience. By prioritizing conflict resolution, leaders demonstrate their commitment to fostering an environment where conflicts are addressed proactively, differences are respected, and relationships are nurtured. **Ultimately, adept conflict resolution empowers leaders to navigate the** complexities of organizational dynamics, driving productivity, innovation, and success both within and beyond the organization's walls.

VIII. Emotional Intelligence in Leadership

Emotional intelligence (EI) is paramount in leadership due to its profound impact on interpersonal dynamics, decision-making, and overall organizational effectiveness. **Leaders with high emotional intelligence possess the ability to understand, manage, and leverage emotions effectively, both in themselves and in others.** This enables them to communicate with clarity, empathy, and authenticity, fostering trust, collaboration, and engagement within their teams.

Emotionally intelligent leaders also excel in building strong and positive relationships, as they are adept at recognizing and responding to the emotions and needs of their team members. They can navigate conflicts and challenges with resilience and grace, fostering a culture of open communication, respect, and mutual support. Additionally, emotional intelligence influences leaders' decision-making processes, enabling them to consider the emotional impact of their decisions on others and make more informed and inclusive choices.

Emotionally intelligent leaders inspire and motivate their teams by articulating a compelling vision, providing encouragement and support, and recognizing and appreciating individual contributions. Overall, emotional intelligence is essential for effective leadership as it enables leaders to navigate complexities, build trust and rapport, inspire, and motivate others, and drive organizational success in today's dynamic and interconnected business landscape.

A. Recognizing and Managing Emotions

An empathetic leader possesses the ability to recognize and manage the emotions of their team members effectively, fostering a supportive and productive work environment. **Recognizing and managing emotions involves being attuned to both verbal and nonverbal cues, understanding the underlying causes and implications of emotions, and responding appropriately to support the well-being and performance of team members.**

Firstly, a leader with high EI is attentive and empathetic, actively listening to their team members and paying attention to their verbal and nonverbal cues. By observing facial expressions, body language, and tone of voice, leaders can gain insights into the emotional states of their team members and discern their needs and concerns. **They create a safe and inclusive space where team members feel comfortable expressing their emotions openly and honestly, without fear of judgment or reprisal.**

Secondly, a leader with high EI is skilled in empathy, understanding, and validating the emotions of their team members. They demonstrate empathy by acknowledging and validating the feelings and experiences of others, showing genuine concern, and understanding, and offering support and encouragement when needed. **By validating emotions, leaders help team members feel heard, understood, and valued, fostering trust and rapport within the team.**

Thirdly, a leader with high EI is adept at managing emotions effectively, both in themselves and in others. They remain calm and composed under pressure, modeling emotional regulation and resilience for their team members. They provide guidance and support to help team members navigate their emotions constructively, offering perspective, reassurance, and practical solutions when needed. **By addressing emotions proactively and constructively, leaders prevent conflicts, reduce stress, and promote psychological safety within the team.**

An empathetic leader creates opportunities for emotional expression and reflection within the team, fostering self-awareness and emotional intelligence among team members. They encourage open communication, honest feedback, and vulnerability, creating a culture where emotions are acknowledged and valued as an integral part of the human experience.

Additionally, they provide resources and support for personal and professional development, such as coaching, training, and counseling, to help team members enhance their emotional intelligence and resilience over time.

A leader with high EI recognizes and manages the emotions of their team members effectively by being attentive, empathetic, and skilled in emotional regulation. **By creating a safe and inclusive space for emotional expression, validating the feelings of others, and offering support and guidance when needed, leaders foster trust, collaboration, and psychological safety within the team.** Also, by promoting self-awareness and emotional intelligence, leaders empower team members to navigate their emotions constructively and achieve their full potential in the workplace.

B. Connecting with Others on a Human Level

Connecting with your team on a human level as a leader is essential for building trust, fostering engagement, and creating a positive work environment. When leaders demonstrate empathy, authenticity, and genuine care for their team members, it strengthens the bond between them and promotes a sense of belonging and loyalty within the team. There are several key reasons why connecting with your team on a human level is important:

1. **Builds Trust:** Connecting with your team on a human level builds trust and rapport, as it demonstrates that you value and respect them as individuals, not just employees. By showing empathy, listening actively, and understanding their needs and concerns, you create a supportive and open environment where team members feel comfortable sharing their thoughts, ideas, and challenges.

2. **Enhances Communication:** When leaders connect with their team members on a human level and shows their true colors, it enhances communication and collaboration within the team. Team members are more likely to express themselves openly and honestly when they feel understood and valued by their leader. This leads to clearer, more effective communication, fewer misunderstandings, and better alignment towards common goals.

3. **Fosters Engagement:** Connecting with your team on a human level fosters greater engagement and commitment among team members. When leaders demonstrate empathy, authenticity, and transparency, it creates a sense of connection and purpose that motivates team members to give their best effort and contribute to the success of the team and organization.

4. **Promotes Well-being:** Building connections with your team on a human level promotes well-being and resilience among team members. When leaders show genuine care and concern for their team members' personal and professional growth, it creates a supportive and nurturing environment where individuals feel valued, supported, and empowered to thrive.

5. **Drives Performance:** Ultimately, connecting with your team on a human level drives performance and productivity within the team. When team members feel valued, respected, and supported by their leader, they are more likely to be motivated, engaged, and committed to achieving their goals. This leads to higher levels of job satisfaction, lower turnover rates, and better overall performance for the team and organization.

Connecting with your team on a human level is essential for building trust, fostering engagement, promoting well-being, and driving performance within the team. **By demonstrating empathy, authenticity, and genuine care for your team members, you create a positive work environment where individuals feel valued, supported, and empowered to achieve their full potential.**

C. Effectiveness of Strong Team Camaraderie

Team camaraderie is crucial in business as it fosters a sense of unity, collaboration, and mutual support among team members, ultimately leading to improved morale, productivity, and performance. **When team members feel connected to one another and share a common sense of purpose, they are more likely to work together harmoniously, communicate effectively, and leverage each other's strengths to achieve shared goals.** There are several reasons why team camaraderie is important in business:

1. **Boosts Morale:** A strong sense of camaraderie boosts morale within the team, leading to greater job satisfaction and overall happiness among team members. When individuals feel supported, appreciated, and valued by their peers, they are more motivated to perform at their best and take pride in their work.

2. **Fosters Collaboration:** Camaraderie promotes collaboration and teamwork within the team, as team members are more willing to share ideas, resources, and feedback with one another. When individuals trust and respect their colleagues, they are more likely to collaborate effectively, resolve conflicts constructively, and achieve better outcomes together.

3. **Improves Communication:** Team camaraderie improves communication and interpersonal relationships within the team, leading to clearer, more effective communication and fewer misunderstandings or conflicts. When individuals feel comfortable and supported by their peers, they are more likely to communicate openly, honestly, and respectfully, leading to better alignment and coordination towards common goals.

4. **Increases Productivity:** A cohesive team with strong camaraderie tends to be more productive, as team members are motivated to support one another, share responsibilities, and work towards shared objectives.

When individuals feel a sense of belonging and connection with their team, they are more engaged, committed, and focused on achieving success together.

5. **Enhances Resilience:** Team camaraderie enhances resilience and adaptability within the team, as individuals are more likely to support and encourage one another during challenging times. When faced with setbacks or obstacles, team members can draw strength and motivation from their shared sense of camaraderie, enabling them to overcome challenges with greater confidence and perseverance.

A good leader plays a crucial role in promoting team camaraderie and fostering a positive team culture. Here are some ways a leader can help promote camaraderie within their team:

1. **Lead by Example:** A good leader sets the tone for teamwork and collaboration by demonstrating camaraderie and respect towards their team members. By modeling positive behavior and treating team members with fairness, kindness, and empathy, leaders inspire trust, respect, and camaraderie within the team.

2. **Encourage Collaboration:** Leaders can encourage collaboration and teamwork by creating opportunities for team members to work together on projects, share ideas, and collaborate towards common goals. By fostering a collaborative environment where every voice is heard and valued, leaders promote a sense of camaraderie and unity within the team.

3. **Promote Open Communication:** Leaders should promote open communication and transparency within the team, encouraging team members to share their thoughts, ideas, and concerns openly and

honestly. By creating a safe and inclusive space for communication, leaders foster trust, respect, and camaraderie among team members.

4. **Recognize and Appreciate Contributions:** Leaders should recognize and appreciate the contributions and achievements of their team members, celebrating successes and milestones together. By acknowledging individual and team accomplishments, leaders reinforce a sense of camaraderie and pride within the team, motivating team members to continue working together towards shared goals.

5. **Invest in Team Building:** Leaders can invest in team building activities and initiatives to strengthen bonds and foster camaraderie among team members. Whether it's through team outings, retreats, or workshops, leaders provide opportunities for team members to connect, build relationships, and have fun together outside of work.

Team camaraderie is essential in business as it promotes unity, collaboration, and mutual support among team members, leading to improved morale, productivity, and performance. A leader with high EI plays a critical role in promoting camaraderie within their team by leading by example, encouraging collaboration, promoting open communication, recognizing contributions, and investing in team building activities. By fostering a positive team culture built on trust, respect, and camaraderie, leaders create an environment where individuals feel valued, supported, and empowered to achieve success together.

D. Bouncing Back from Adversity

Being a resilient leader and bouncing back from adversity can lead to better results in various ways. **Resilient leaders inspire confidence among their team members by demonstrating strength, optimism, and determination in the face of challenges.** When team members see their leader remain composed and positive despite setbacks, it reassures them that obstacles can be overcome, instilling a sense of hope and motivation to persevere. This confidence boosts morale and engagement, encouraging team members to stay committed and focused on achieving their goals even in difficult times.

Resilient leaders also maintain focus on their goals and priorities, preventing setbacks from derailing progress or causing unnecessary delays. By staying composed and level-headed under pressure, resilient leaders can guide their teams through adversity with clarity and purpose. They provide direction and support, helping team members stay on track and navigate obstacles effectively. This steadfast focus enables the team to stay aligned and productive, even in the face of challenges and uncertainty.

A resilient leader promotes adaptability and innovation within their teams, encouraging creative problem-solving and experimentation to overcome obstacles and seize new opportunities. Rather than being discouraged by setbacks, resilient leaders see them as opportunities for growth and improvement. They encourage team members to think outside the box, explore new approaches, and take calculated risks to drive innovation and achieve better results. This culture of innovation fosters resilience and agility within the team, enabling them to thrive in a rapidly changing business environment.

Additionally, resilient leaders build trust and loyalty among team members by demonstrating integrity, empathy, and authenticity in their actions. When leaders are transparent and honest about challenges and setbacks, it fosters a sense of trust and respect within the team. Team members feel valued and supported, knowing that their leader has their best interests at heart. This trust and loyalty create a strong foundation for collaboration and teamwork, enabling the team to overcome adversity together and achieve shared goals.

A resilient leader can view setbacks and failures as opportunities for learning and growth, encouraging reflection, adaptation, and personal development among their teams. **Rather than dwelling on mistakes or shortcomings, resilient leaders encourage team members to learn from them and use them as steppingstones to future success.** They provide support and guidance, helping team members identify areas for improvement and develop new skills. This focus on continuous learning and growth fosters resilience and self-confidence within the team, empowering them to overcome challenges and achieve better results in the future.

IX. Decision-Making and Problem-Solving

Decision-making and problem-solving stand as cornerstone leadership qualities indispensable for guiding organizations through challenges and achieving strategic objectives. These competencies enable leaders to navigate complexities, capitalize on opportunities, and drive organizational success effectively. Effective decision-making entails aligning actions with the organization's long-term vision, strategic priorities, and values. **Leaders must analyze information, evaluate alternatives, and consider potential outcomes to make informed decisions that drive progress and ensure alignment with organizational goals.** Skilled problem-solving skills empower leaders to address complex issues, overcome obstacles, and capitalize on opportunities effectively. Leaders identify root causes, assess risks, and develop strategies to mitigate them, fostering a culture of innovation and adaptability within the organization.

In today's dynamic and fast-paced business environment, the ability to make timely and sound decisions is paramount for leaders. The decisions leaders make impact not only their immediate team but also the entire organization. Effective decision making enables leaders to navigate uncertainties, capitalize on opportunities, and mitigate risks effectively. **By considering various perspectives, weighing alternatives, and anticipating potential outcomes, leaders can make informed decisions that drive organizational success and create value for stakeholders.**

Similarly, skilled problem-solving skills are essential for leaders to address challenges, capitalize on opportunities, and drive innovation within the organization. **In the face of complexity and uncertainty, leaders must be able to identify root causes, analyze data, and develop creative solutions to overcome obstacles effectively.** Moreover, effective problem-solving enables leaders to foster a culture of innovation and adaptability within the organization, encouraging team members to think critically, challenge the status quo, and explore new approaches to achieving organizational goals.

Furthermore, decision making and problem-solving are essential for managing conflicts, allocating resources efficiently, and engaging team members effectively. **By involving team members in decision-making processes and problem-solving activities, leaders cultivate collaboration, ownership, and commitment, enhancing organizational performance and morale.** Effective decision making and problem-solving enable leaders to build trust and credibility with their team members, inspiring confidence, and loyalty in their leadership.

When team members see their leaders making informed decisions and addressing challenges effectively, it fosters a sense of trust, respect, and confidence in their leadership abilities. This trust and credibility are essential for building strong relationships and fostering collaboration within the team, leading to better performance and results.

Timely decision making and problem-solving are critical leadership qualities that enable leaders to navigate complexities, capitalize on opportunities, and drive organizational success effectively. By making informed decisions, addressing challenges, and fostering a culture of innovation and adaptability, leaders inspire confidence, build trust, and achieve better results for the organization.

A. Making Informed Decisions for Long-Term Success

Strategic thinking empowers leaders to anticipate future challenges, capitalize on opportunities, and drive long-term success for their organizations. By adopting a strategic mindset, leaders can align their actions with the organization's long-term vision and goals, anticipate changes in the business environment, and develop proactive strategies to navigate uncertainties effectively. Here's how strategic thinking makes a leader more effective for long-term success:

1. **Visionary Leadership:** Strategic thinking enables leaders to articulate a compelling vision for the future and inspire others to rally behind it. By envisioning where the organization wants to be in the long term, leaders can set clear goals and priorities that guide decision making and resource allocation, ensuring alignment with the organization's strategic objectives.

2. **Anticipating Trends and Opportunities:** Strategic thinking allows leaders to scan the business environment, identify emerging trends, and anticipate future opportunities and threats. By staying abreast of industry developments, technological advancements, and market trends, leaders can position their organizations to capitalize on opportunities and mitigate risks effectively, driving sustainable growth and competitive advantage.

3. **Setting Direction and Priorities:** Strategic thinking enables leaders to set direction and priorities that drive organizational success over the long term. By defining strategic objectives, establishing key performance indicators (KPIs), and developing action plans, leaders provide clarity and direction for their teams, ensuring that everyone is aligned and focused on achieving common goals.

4. **Allocating Resources Effectively:** Strategic thinking empowers leaders to allocate resources—such as budget, talent, and time—effectively to support long-term objectives. By prioritizing investments in areas that align with the organization's strategic priorities and offer the greatest potential for return on investment, leaders optimize resource utilization and drive sustainable growth and profitability.

5. **Driving Innovation and Adaptation:** Strategic thinking fosters a culture of innovation and adaptation within the organization, encouraging creativity, experimentation, and continuous improvement. By encouraging employees to think critically, challenge the status quo, and

explore new ideas and approaches, leaders drive innovation and ensure that their organizations remain agile and responsive to changing market dynamics.

6. **Building Resilience and Sustainability:** Strategic thinking enables leaders to build resilience and sustainability into their organizations, ensuring their ability to thrive in the face of challenges and uncertainties. By developing contingency plans, diversifying revenue streams, and building strategic partnerships, leaders mitigate risks and enhance their organizations' ability to withstand disruptions and emerge stronger from adversity.

7. **Monitoring and Adjusting Strategies:** Strategic thinking involves continuous monitoring and evaluation of progress towards strategic objectives, as well as adjusting strategies in response to changing circumstances. By regularly reviewing performance metrics, soliciting feedback, and conducting strategic reviews, leaders can identify areas for improvement, make course corrections as needed, and ensure that their organizations remain on track to achieve long-term success.

By envisioning the future, anticipating trends and opportunities, setting direction and priorities, allocating resources effectively, driving innovation and adaptation, building resilience and sustainability, and monitoring and adjusting strategies, leaders can navigate uncertainties and challenges effectively, ensuring that their organizations remain competitive, agile, and successful in the long run.

B. Adapting to Change and Leading Through Challenges

Leading through uncertainty and adapting to change are essential skills for leaders to navigate challenges effectively and drive organizational success. In times of uncertainty, such as during periods of economic instability, technological disruption, or global crises, leaders must demonstrate resilience, agility, and adaptability to steer their organizations through turbulent waters. Here's how leading through uncertainty and adapting to change help a leader lead through challenges:

1. **Maintain Stability and Calm:** During times of uncertainty, leaders must maintain stability and calm to reassure their teams and stakeholders. By demonstrating composure, confidence, and clear communication, leaders instill a sense of trust and confidence in their ability to navigate challenges and lead the organization through uncertainty effectively.

2. **Fostering Resilience:** Leading through uncertainty requires resilience—the ability to bounce back from setbacks, overcome obstacles, and persevere in the face of adversity. Resilient leaders inspire resilience in their teams by modeling perseverance, optimism, and adaptability, encouraging team members to stay focused, motivated, and agile in the face of challenges.

3. **Embracing Change:** Adapting to change is essential for leaders to thrive in uncertain environments. Leaders must embrace change as an opportunity for growth and innovation, rather than a threat to the status quo. By fostering a culture of continuous learning, experimentation, and adaptation, leaders empower their teams to embrace change, seize opportunities, and drive organizational success.

4. **Anticipating and Mitigating Risks:** Leading through uncertainty requires leaders to anticipate and mitigate risks effectively. Leaders must assess the potential impact of external factors, such as economic downturns, market fluctuations, or regulatory changes, on their organizations and develop strategies to mitigate risks and protect against adverse consequences.

5. **Driving Innovation and Creativity:** Uncertain times often present opportunities for innovation and creativity. Leaders must encourage a culture of innovation within their organizations, empowering team members to think outside the box, challenge the status quo, and explore new ideas and approaches to solving problems. By fostering a culture of innovation, leaders drive organizational agility and resilience, enabling their organizations to adapt and thrive in changing environments.

6. **Communicating Effectively:** Effective communication is critical for leading through uncertainty. Leaders must keep their teams informed, engaged, and motivated by providing regular updates, transparent communication, and clear direction. By communicating openly and honestly about challenges, opportunities, and expectations, leaders foster trust, alignment, and collaboration within their teams.

7. **Empowering and Supporting Teams:** Leading through uncertainty requires leaders to empower and support their teams to navigate challenges effectively. Leaders must provide the resources, guidance, and support necessary for their teams to succeed, while also empowering them to take ownership of their work, make decisions autonomously, and adapt to changing circumstances.

Leading through uncertainty and adapting to change are essential skills for leaders to navigate challenges effectively and drive organizational success. By maintaining stability and calm, fostering resilience, embracing change, anticipating, and mitigating risks, driving innovation and creativity, communicating effectively, and empowering and supporting their teams, leaders can lead their organizations through uncertain times with confidence and resilience, ensuring long-term success and sustainability.

C. Turning Setbacks into Opportunities for Growth

Leveraging failure to turn setbacks into opportunities for growth is a profound leadership strategy that cultivates resilience, innovation, and continuous improvement within teams. In today's dynamic and uncertain business landscape, leaders must navigate challenges effectively, and failure can serve as a powerful catalyst for learning and growth. By adopting a strategic approach to failure, leaders can foster a culture where setbacks are viewed not as roadblocks but as steppingstones toward success. Here's how leaders can leverage failure to drive growth within their teams:

Firstly, leaders must normalize failure by creating a safe environment where team members feel comfortable taking risks and experimenting without fear of judgment or reprisal. Acknowledging their own failures and setbacks, leaders set the tone for open and honest communication, encouraging team members to share their experiences and learn from each other's mistakes. By destigmatizing failure, leaders create a culture that values innovation, resilience, and continuous learning.

Secondly, leaders should encourage reflection and learning from failure by prompting team members to analyze what went wrong and identify valuable lessons that can be applied in the future. Through post-mortem discussions and debriefs, leaders facilitate a process of collective introspection, enabling teams to extract insights, identify root causes, and develop actionable strategies for improvement. By asking questions such as "What did we learn from this?" and "How can we do better next time?", leaders stimulate critical thinking and promote a growth mindset within their teams.

Leaders must also promote a growth mindset within their teams, emphasizing that abilities and intelligence can be developed through effort and perseverance. **By praising effort, resilience, and the willingness to take on challenges, leaders cultivate a mindset of optimism and resilience that empowers team members to embrace failure as an opportunity for growth and development.** By reframing failure as a natural part of the learning process, leaders empower their teams to view setbacks not as personal shortcomings but as valuable learning experiences that contribute to their growth and development.

Additionally, leaders should provide support and constructive feedback to help team members learn from failure and improve their performance. By offering guidance, coaching, and mentorship, leaders demonstrate their commitment to their team's success and well-being, fostering a culture of trust, collaboration, and mutual support. Through empathetic listening and targeted interventions, leaders help team members overcome obstacles, address challenges, and develop the skills and competencies needed to succeed in their roles.

Leaders must celebrate progress and successes, no matter how small, to reinforce positive behaviors and attitudes among team members. By recognizing and celebrating achievements, leaders boost team morale, motivation, and confidence, creating a positive feedback loop that encourages continued effort and engagement. By highlighting examples of resilience, innovation, and perseverance, leaders inspire their teams to persevere through adversity and strive for excellence in everything they do.

Finally, leaders should create opportunities for growth and development, such as challenging projects, stretch targets, and cross-functional collaborations. By providing opportunities for team members to apply what they've learned from failure and contribute to the organization's success, leaders empower their teams to take ownership of their work, make decisions autonomously, and drive positive change within the organization. Through experiential learning and hands-on experience, team members develop the skills, competencies, and confidence needed to succeed in their roles and advance their careers.

Leveraging failure to turn setbacks into opportunities for growth is a powerful leadership strategy that fosters resilience, innovation, and continuous improvement within teams. By normalizing failure, encouraging reflection and learning, promoting a growth mindset, providing support and feedback, celebrating progress and successes, leading by example, and creating opportunities for growth, leaders can empower their teams to embrace failure as a natural part of the learning process and achieve greater success in the long run.

X. The Diversity of Leadership Styles

Leadership styles vary widely, reflecting the diverse approaches that leaders employ to inspire, motivate, and guide their teams. These styles are shaped by a leader's personality, values, experiences, and the context in which they operate. In this section, we will explore some of the most common leadership styles, their characteristics, strengths, weaknesses, and when they are most effective. I'll also provide a famous business leader that embodies that style for reference.

1. **Autocratic Leadership**: Autocratic leadership is characterized by centralized decision-making, with the leader holding all authority and control. In this style, the leader dictates tasks, sets goals, and expects compliance without input from subordinates. Autocratic leaders make decisions quickly and enforce strict adherence to rules and procedures.

Strengths:

- Clear direction: Autocratic leaders provide clear instructions and expectations, minimizing ambiguity.

- Rapid decision-making: With authority centralized, decisions can be made quickly without the need for consultation.

- Strong leadership in crises: In emergency situations or times of uncertainty, autocratic leadership can provide stability and direction.

Weaknesses:

- Lack of employee involvement: Employees may feel disengaged and demotivated when their input is disregarded.

- Creativity stifled: The rigid structure and limited autonomy can inhibit innovation and creativity.

- Employee dissatisfaction: Micromanagement and lack of autonomy can lead to low morale and high turnover rates.

      A famous autocratic business leader is Henry Ford, the founder of the Ford Motor Company. Ford was known for his authoritarian leadership style, which was characterized by centralized decision-making and strict control over all aspects of the company's operations. He famously introduced the assembly line production method, revolutionizing the manufacturing industry and making cars more affordable to the masses. Ford's autocratic leadership approach enabled him to maintain tight control over the production process and ensure consistency in product quality. However, his leadership style also led to clashes with labor unions and criticism for his treatment of workers, including his opposition to unionization and his use of harsh tactics to suppress dissent. Despite these controversies, Ford's innovative contributions to the automotive industry and his role in popularizing the concept of mass production have left a lasting legacy. His autocratic leadership style played a significant role in shaping the modern business landscape and influencing generations of entrepreneurs and business leaders.

2. **Democratic Leadership**: Democratic leadership, also known as participative leadership, emphasizes collaboration, inclusion, and shared decision-making. In this style, the leader seeks input and feedback from employees, encouraging open communication and fostering a sense of ownership and responsibility.

Strengths:

- Increased employee engagement: By involving employees in decision-making, democratic leaders empower them and foster a sense of ownership.

- Enhanced creativity and innovation: Employees feel valued and motivated to contribute ideas and solutions, driving innovation.

- Higher job satisfaction: Employees appreciate being heard and having a say in decisions that affect them, leading to higher levels of job satisfaction and commitment.

Weaknesses:

- Time-consuming: Seeking input from multiple stakeholders can be time-consuming and may slow down the decision-making process.

- Consensus may not always be reached: In situations where consensus cannot be reached, decisions may be delayed or compromised.

- Not suitable for all situations: In emergencies or situations requiring decisive action, democratic leadership may be less effective.

A famous democratic business leader is Bill Gates, the co-founder of Microsoft Corporation. Gates is known for his collaborative and inclusive leadership style, which emphasized teamwork, innovation, and employee empowerment. He fostered a culture of open communication and idea-sharing within Microsoft, encouraging employees to collaborate across departments and divisions to drive innovation and solve complex problems. Gates was also known for his commitment to philanthropy and social responsibility, using his wealth and influence to address global challenges such as poverty, disease, and education. Under his leadership, Microsoft became one of the world's leading technology companies, pioneering groundbreaking products and services that have transformed industries and changed the way people work, communicate, and live. Gates' democratic leadership approach helped Microsoft attract and retain top talent, foster a culture of innovation and creativity, and achieve sustainable growth and success over the years.

3. **Transformational Leadership**: Transformational leadership focuses on inspiring and motivating followers to achieve extraordinary outcomes. Transformational leaders articulate a compelling vision, challenge the status quo, and empower employees to reach their full potential. They lead by example, fostering a culture of trust, innovation, and continuous improvement.

Strengths:

- Inspires motivation and commitment: Transformational leaders inspire and motivate employees to go above and beyond, driving performance and achieving exceptional results.

- Promotes organizational change: By challenging the status quo and articulating a compelling vision, transformational leaders drive organizational change and foster a culture of innovation.

- Develops future leaders: Transformational leaders invest in developing the skills and capabilities of their employees, cultivating a pipeline of future leaders.

Weaknesses:

- Relies heavily on charisma: Transformational leaders often rely on charisma and personality to inspire others, which may not be replicable or sustainable for all leaders.

- Resistance to change: Some employees may resist the changes advocated by transformational leaders, leading to conflicts and resistance.

- Potential for burnout: The high expectations and demands placed on transformational leaders can lead to burnout if not managed effectively.

A famous transformational business leader is Jeff Bezos, the founder and former CEO of Amazon. Bezos is widely recognized for his visionary leadership style, which has transformed Amazon from an online bookstore into one of the world's largest and most influential technology companies. Bezos' transformational leadership is evident in his relentless focus on innovation, customer obsession, and long-term thinking. He has consistently pushed the boundaries of what is possible, pioneering new technologies and business models that have disrupted traditional industries and reshaped the way people shop, consume media, and conduct business. Bezos' bold vision and willingness to take risks have been instrumental in driving Amazon's growth and success, enabling the company to diversify into a wide range of businesses, including cloud computing, artificial intelligence, and entertainment. Additionally, Bezos' commitment to a culture of experimentation and continuous improvement has fostered a spirit of innovation and entrepreneurship within Amazon, empowering employees to explore new ideas and pursue ambitious goals. Overall, Jeff Bezos exemplifies the qualities of a transformational leader through his visionary leadership, innovative mindset, and relentless pursuit of excellence, making him one of the most influential business leaders of the modern era.

4. **Transactional Leadership**: Transactional leadership is based on the exchange of rewards and punishments for performance. In this style, leaders establish clear expectations, set goals, and provide rewards for meeting objectives while administering discipline for failure to meet expectations.

Strengths:

- Clear expectations: Transactional leaders provide clear guidelines and expectations, ensuring that employees understand what is required of them.

- Accountability: By linking rewards to performance, transactional leaders hold employees accountable for their actions and outcomes.

- Effective in stable environments: Transactional leadership can be effective in stable environments where routine tasks and clear procedures are essential.

Weaknesses:

- Limited motivation: Transactional leadership relies on extrinsic motivators such as rewards and punishments, which may not be sufficient to inspire higher levels of performance or commitment.

- Inhibits creativity: The focus on following established procedures and meeting objectives can stifle creativity and innovation.

- Reliance on authority: Transactional leaders rely on their authority to enforce compliance, which may lead to resentment or resistance among employees.

A famous transactional leader is Jack Welch, the former CEO of General Electric (GE). Welch is widely recognized for his pragmatic and results-oriented leadership style, which focused on setting clear goals, establishing performance metrics, and rewarding high achievers. As CEO of GE from 1981 to 2001, Welch implemented a series of aggressive cost-cutting measures and organizational restructuring initiatives that transformed the company into one of the world's most successful and admired conglomerates. Welch emphasized accountability and performance, instituting a rigorous performance review system known as "rank and yank," which rewarded top performers with promotions and bonuses while weeding out underperformers. Under Welch's leadership, GE experienced significant growth in revenue and market capitalization, with its stock price increasing by over 4,000% during his tenure. While Welch's leadership approach was criticized for its emphasis on short-term results and its impact on employee morale, there is no denying the significant impact he had on GE and the broader business world. His transactional leadership style helped drive performance and profitability at GE, making him one of the most influential business leaders of his time.

5. **Servant Leadership**: Servant leadership emphasizes serving others, putting the needs of followers first, and empowering them to achieve their full potential. Servant leaders prioritize empathy, compassion, and humility, seeking to build strong relationships and support the growth and development of their teams.

Strengths:

- Empowers employees: Servant leaders empower employees to take ownership of their work, make decisions, and contribute to the organization's success.

- Builds trust and loyalty: By prioritizing the needs of others and demonstrating empathy and compassion, servant leaders build strong relationships based on trust and loyalty.

- Promotes a culture of collaboration: Servant leaders foster a culture of collaboration, teamwork, and mutual respect, where employees feel valued and supported.

Weaknesses:

- Misunderstood or exploited: Servant leaders may be misunderstood or exploited by employees who take advantage of their generosity or willingness to serve.

- Slow decision-making: Servant leaders prioritize consensus-building and employee development, which may slow down the decision-making process, especially in fast-paced environments.

- Not suitable for all situations: Servant leadership may not be effective in situations requiring decisive action or strong leadership in crises.

A famous servant business leader is Herb Kelleher, the co-founder and former CEO of Southwest Airlines. Kelleher is renowned for his servant leadership approach, which prioritized the well-being of employees and customers above all else. He believed that by taking care of employees, they would in turn take care of customers, leading to business success. Kelleher fostered a culture of mutual respect, trust, and empowerment within Southwest Airlines, where employees were encouraged to voice their opinions and contribute ideas. He famously said, "Your employees come first, and if you treat them right, they'll treat your customers right." Under Kelleher's leadership, Southwest Airlines became known for its exceptional customer service, low fares, and strong employee morale. Kelleher's servant leadership approach contributed to Southwest's success as a leading airline and earned him widespread recognition as one of the most admired and respected business leaders in the world. His legacy continues to inspire leaders across industries to prioritize people and values in their leadership approach.

6. **Laissez-Faire Leadership:** Laissez-faire leadership, also known as hands-off leadership, involves minimal intervention or direction from the leader. In this style, employees are given autonomy and freedom to make decisions and manage their own work with minimal oversight from the leader.

Strengths:

- Promotes autonomy and creativity: Laissez-faire leadership empowers employees to take ownership of their work, make decisions, and explore creative solutions to problems.

- Fosters innovation: Employees are encouraged to experiment, take risks, and explore new ideas without fear of micromanagement or interference.

- Develops self-reliance: Laissez-faire leadership encourages employees to develop self-reliance, problem-solving skills, and initiative, which can lead to increased confidence and competence.

Weaknesses:

- Lack of direction: Without clear direction or guidance from the leader, employees may feel adrift or uncertain about their roles and responsibilities.

- Potential for chaos: In the absence of leadership oversight, there is a risk that teams may become disorganized, inefficient, or unproductive.

- Limited accountability: Laissez-faire leadership can lead to a lack of accountability, as employees may not feel responsible for their actions or outcomes without leadership guidance or supervision.

A famous laissez-faire business leader is Tony Hsieh, the former CEO of Zappos. Hsieh was known for his hands-off management style, which empowered employees to take ownership of their work and make decisions autonomously. He famously implemented a "Holacracy" organizational structure at Zappos, which decentralized authority and encouraged self-management among employees. Hsieh believed in giving employees the freedom to innovate and experiment, trusting that they would act in the best interest of the company. Under his leadership, Zappos became known for its unique company culture and exceptional customer service, earning numerous accolades and awards. Hsieh's laissez-faire leadership approach contributed to Zappos' success as a leading online retailer and solidified his reputation as a visionary entrepreneur.

Leadership styles vary widely, each with its own strengths, weaknesses, and suitability for different situations. Autocratic leadership provides clear direction and rapid decision-making but may stifle creativity and employee engagement. Democratic leadership fosters collaboration and innovation but may be time-consuming and less effective in emergencies. Transformational leadership inspires motivation and organizational change but may rely too heavily on charisma and be susceptible to burnout. Transactional leadership establishes clear expectations and accountability but may inhibit creativity and intrinsic motivation. Servant leadership prioritizes the needs of others and builds trust but may be misunderstood or exploited by employees. Laissez-faire leadership promotes autonomy and creativity but may lack direction and accountability.

Ultimately, effective leaders adapt their leadership style to suit the needs of their team, the demands of the situation, and the organizational context, drawing on a range of leadership approaches to inspire, motivate, and guide their teams to success. I truly believe that leaders who can modify their leadership style to the individuals on the team or the situations they face, will be dramatically more successful than a one sticks with one style and makes others conform to it.

A. The Correlation Between Successful Athletes and Strong Leadership

Athletes and strong business leaders share numerous qualities that contribute to their success, demonstrating a remarkable correlation between the worlds of sports and business. While their arenas may differ, the traits and characteristics they exhibit are remarkably similar, highlighting the universal principles of achievement and excellence.

Resilience stands out as a defining trait shared by athletes and business leaders alike. Athletes face numerous challenges throughout their careers, from injuries to defeats, yet they bounce back with unwavering determination. This resilience enables them to overcome adversity, learn from setbacks, and emerge stronger and more determined. Similarly, strong business leaders display resilience in the face of obstacles and setbacks. They navigate turbulent markets, economic downturns, and competitive pressures with poise and determination, viewing challenges as opportunities for growth and learning.

Determination and work ethic are other fundamental traits shared by athletes and business leaders. Athletes set ambitious goals and work tirelessly to achieve them, pushing themselves beyond their limits to reach new heights of performance. Their relentless pursuit of success drives them to train harder, push through pain, and persevere in the face of adversity. Likewise, strong business leaders exhibit a relentless commitment to achieving their goals and objectives. They set ambitious targets, rally their teams, and drive performance with unwavering focus and dedication. Their determination fuels their drive for success, inspiring others to excel and achieve greatness.

Strategic thinking is a critical skill that both athletes and business leaders possess. Athletes analyze their opponents, assess their strengths and weaknesses, and devise winning strategies to secure victory. They anticipate challenges, adapt to changing circumstances, and execute their game plan with precision and agility. Similarly, strong business leaders employ strategic thinking to navigate the complexities of the business world. They analyze market trends, assess competitive threats, and anticipate changes in the business landscape to stay ahead of the curve. Their ability to think strategically enables them to identify opportunities, mitigate risks, and make informed decisions that drive sustainable growth and success.

Teamwork is another essential trait that athletes and business leaders share. Athletes understand the importance of collaboration, communication, and trust in achieving collective goals. They work closely with their teammates, support each other, and leverage their strengths to achieve success as a team. Likewise, strong business leaders recognize the value of teamwork and foster a culture of collaboration within their organizations. They empower their teams, encourage open communication, and leverage the diverse talents and perspectives of their employees to drive innovation and achieve shared objectives. By fostering a culture of teamwork, they create a cohesive and high-performing organization that can achieve greatness together.

Adaptability is another crucial trait shared by athletes and business leaders. Athletes must adapt to changing conditions, opponents, and game plans, constantly adjusting their strategies and tactics to stay ahead. Similarly, strong business leaders must adapt to evolving market dynamics, technological advancements, and customer preferences. They embrace change, anticipate disruptions, and pivot quickly to capitalize on new opportunities and mitigate risks. By remaining agile and adaptable, they can navigate uncertainty and thrive in a rapidly changing environment.

Coachability is an important trait. As an athlete you are constantly getting feedback and direction from coaches. This back and forth is the foundation in sports. There are zero percent of professional athletes that get to where they are by themselves. They have personal trainers, head coaches, assistant coaches, nutritionists, etc. They are surrounded by professionals who are all trying to make that athlete more successful. It should not be any different in the professional business world. If you are someone who can take constructive criticism and apply it to make you better, you'll be more successful than others. In addition, you'll be more of a pleasure to work with and your managers will appreciate that you care about what they are saying to help you. You should always be trying to get feedback from your peers and managers.

Sports is flooded with **failure**. Losing games, striking out, missing a shot, putting the ball in the water, getting an error, getting knocked down, failing to qualify. There is no shortage of failure, however, an elite athlete learns from their mistakes and try to minimize future errors or improve. In business, mistakes are made, performance metrics fall short, employees show up late, projects are lost, tasks take longer than they should. Successful leaders help their employees by providing constructive feedback so they can learn from those mistakes and be better.

Overall leadership is the most significant quality that often emerges naturally in both athletes and business leaders. Athletes lead by example, inspiring their teammates with their passion, dedication, and work ethic. They set the tone for their team, motivate others to perform at their best, and lead by example on and off the field. Similarly, strong business leaders exhibit exemplary leadership qualities, inspiring and empowering their teams to achieve greatness. They lead with integrity, empathy, and vision, earning the trust and respect of their employees and stakeholders. By leading by example, they create a culture of accountability, excellence, and innovation that drives organizational success.

The most important trait that an athlete has that is important for business is **competitiveness** and the deep-rooted desire to win. Athletes don't like to lose. They honestly spend more time competing with themselves and their teammates than they do with their competition. Two teams compete for the most coveted prize in sports, victory. Each team has the intention of winning, but one group will always prevail, other than ending in a tie of course. In business, you're competing against other companies or competing against yourself by trying to meet the performance metrics that are given to you. As employees, we feel empowered and fulfilled if we were able to accomplish our tasks. Whether we're competing against others or competing against ourselves, that innate desire to not lose or fail is deep rooted in a successful employee. I'm curious to know a company that does not want someone with that competitive attitude leading their team.

The correlation between athletes and strong business leaders is undeniable, as both groups exhibit resilience, determination, strategic thinking, teamwork, leadership, and adaptability. By recognizing the shared traits and characteristics of athletes and business leaders, organizations can leverage these qualities to cultivate a culture of excellence, drive performance, and achieve success in today's competitive landscape. If you are or were an athlete, leverage it, if not, try to embody those traits or hire athletes into your organization.

XI. Leadership Philosophy

Defining your leadership philosophy to your team is a pivotal step towards fostering a cohesive and effective work environment. This process involves articulating the principles, values, and beliefs that guide your leadership approach. By clearly communicating these foundational elements, you establish a framework for how you will lead and interact with your team members.

Defining your leadership philosophy sets clear expectations for your team. **When team members understand the principles and values that underpin your leadership style, they have a better idea of what to expect in terms of behavior, decision-making, and communication.** This clarity helps reduce ambiguity and minimizes misunderstandings, creating a more harmonious and productive working environment.

Sharing your leadership philosophy builds trust and confidence among team members. **Transparency is a key component of effective leadership, and openly communicating your guiding principles demonstrates authenticity and integrity.** Team members are more likely to trust a leader who is transparent about their values and beliefs, fostering a sense of cohesion and unity within the team.

Additionally, defining your leadership philosophy creates a shared vision and sense of purpose within the team. When team members understand the overarching goals and objectives that guide your leadership approach, they feel more connected to the organization's mission and are motivated to contribute towards its success. This shared sense of purpose helps align individual efforts towards common goals, driving greater collaboration and synergy within the team.

Furthermore, **articulating your leadership philosophy promotes accountability within the team.** By outlining the standards of behavior and performance that you expect from yourself and others, you create a culture of accountability where everyone is responsible for upholding the team's values. This accountability fosters a sense of ownership and responsibility among team members, encouraging them to hold themselves and each other to high standards of conduct.

Encouraging open dialogue and feedback is another benefit of defining your leadership philosophy. **When team members understand the principles and values that guide your leadership approach, they are more likely to feel comfortable sharing their thoughts, concerns, and ideas openly.** This open communication fosters a culture of trust and collaboration, where everyone's input is valued and respected.

Remember that defining your leadership philosophy promotes consistency in your leadership with your team. Consistency is essential for building trust and credibility as a leader, as it demonstrates reliability and predictability in your actions and decisions. When team members know what to expect from their leader, they feel more secure and confident in their roles, leading to greater engagement and commitment.

Defining your leadership philosophy to your team is a critical step towards creating a cohesive, high-performing work environment. By articulating the principles, values, and beliefs that guide your leadership approach, you set clear expectations, build trust and confidence, create a shared vision and sense of purpose, promote accountability, encourage open dialogue and feedback, and foster consistency in your leadership style. **Ultimately, a well-defined leadership philosophy empowers your team to succeed by providing them with a clear direction and a strong foundation for collaboration and growth.**

A. Building Trust and Credibility

Building trust and credibility with your team is not just a fundamental aspect of ethical leadership but also a critical factor in the success of any organization. Strong leaders prioritize transparency, integrity, and authenticity in their interactions, creating an environment where trust can thrive. This trust is built through consistent actions and behaviors that align with the leader's stated values and principles. **When leaders communicate openly with their team members, sharing information and insights that help foster understanding and alignment, they demonstrate honesty and integrity.** Transparency in decision-making processes and sharing the rationale behind important choices helps team members feel included and valued, fostering a sense of trust in the leader's judgment.

Consistency and reliability are also key components of building trust and credibility. Leaders adhere to a set of principles and values that guide their actions and decision-making, ensuring that their behavior is predictable and trustworthy. When team members know what to expect from their leader and can rely on them to act with integrity and fairness in all situations, they develop confidence in their leader's abilities and intentions. This consistency helps foster a sense of stability and security within the team, enabling them to focus on their work without worrying about unexpected changes or inconsistencies in leadership behavior.

Furthermore, leaders hold themselves and others accountable for their actions and decisions. They take responsibility for their mistakes and shortcomings, demonstrating humility and integrity. By holding themselves to high standards of conduct and setting clear expectations for their team members, leaders create a culture of accountability where everyone is responsible for upholding the team's values. This accountability fosters a sense of ownership and responsibility among team members, encouraging them to hold themselves and each other to high standards of behavior.

In addition to accountability, leaders show empathy and respect towards their team members. **They listen actively to their concerns, show understanding, and compassion, and treat everyone with dignity and fairness.** By demonstrating empathy and respect, leaders build strong relationships based on trust and mutual respect, creating a supportive and inclusive work environment where team members feel valued and appreciated. This sense of belonging and recognition motivates team members to perform at their best and contribute positively to the team's success.

Leaders prioritize ethical decision-making, considering the potential impact of their decisions on all stakeholders and weighing the consequences carefully. They make decisions based on ethical principles and values, even when it may be difficult or unpopular. By making ethical decisions, leaders demonstrate their commitment to doing what is right, even in challenging situations. This commitment to ethical behavior builds trust and credibility with team members, who appreciate their leader's integrity and honesty.

Finally, building trust and credibility with your team requires investing time and effort in building strong relationships. Effective leaders take the time to get to know their team members, understand their strengths and weaknesses, and support their professional development. **By showing genuine interest in their team members' well-being and growth, leaders demonstrate their commitment to their success and create a sense of loyalty and commitment among team members.** This investment in building relationships based on trust and mutual respect pays dividends in the form of increased engagement, productivity, and retention.

Ethical leaders prioritize transparency, integrity, consistency, accountability, empathy, and ethical decision-making in their interactions with team members. By demonstrating these qualities consistently and investing in building strong relationships, leaders create a supportive and inclusive work environment where trust can thrive. This trust and credibility foster a sense of belonging and commitment among team members, enabling them to work together effectively towards shared goals and objectives. **Ultimately, ethical leadership is not just about doing the right thing—it's also about building relationships based on trust and mutual respect, which are essential for creating a positive and productive work environment.**

B. Inspiring Others to Align with a Shared Vision and Mission

Leaders motivate their teams to follow their vision and mission by effectively communicating the purpose and significance of these goals, inspiring commitment, and alignment among team members, and fostering a supportive and empowering work environment.

Firstly, leaders articulate a compelling vision and mission that resonates with the values and aspirations of their team members. They communicate the broader purpose and significance of the organization's goals, highlighting how they contribute to meaningful outcomes and impact. By painting a vivid picture of the desired future state and the role each team member plays in achieving it, leaders inspire a sense of purpose and motivation among their team.

Secondly, leaders lead by example, demonstrating commitment and passion for the vision and mission. They embody the values and behaviors they expect from their team members, serving as role models and inspiring trust and confidence. By consistently aligning their actions with the organization's goals and values, leaders inspire others to follow suit, creating a culture of accountability and integrity.

Thirdly, leaders empower their teams by providing them with the resources, support, and autonomy they need to succeed. They foster a culture of collaboration and innovation, encouraging team members to share ideas, take risks, and experiment with new approaches. By empowering their teams to take ownership of their work and make meaningful contributions towards the organization's goals, leaders foster a sense of ownership and pride in their achievements.

Furthermore, leaders provide regular feedback and recognition to their team members, acknowledging their contributions and celebrating their successes. They create opportunities for professional growth and development, investing in the skills and capabilities of their team members and helping them realize their full potential. By demonstrating a genuine interest in their team members' well-being and growth, leaders foster a sense of loyalty and commitment among their team members.

Leaders also create a positive and supportive work environment where team members feel valued, respected, and appreciated. They foster open communication and trust, encouraging team members to voice their opinions, share their concerns, and collaborate with one another. By creating a culture of psychological safety and inclusion, leaders empower their teams to challenge the status quo, experiment with new ideas, and drive positive change.

Leaders motivate their teams to follow their vision and mission by effectively communicating the purpose and significance of these goals, leading by example, empowering their teams, providing regular feedback and recognition, investing in their growth and development, and fostering a positive and supportive work environment.

C. Balancing Stakeholder Interests and Team Moral

Making ethical decisions as a leader can have a profoundly positive impact on stakeholder interests and team morale. Ethical decisions are those that are guided by principles of fairness, integrity, and responsibility, and they consider the well-being of all stakeholders involved. When leaders prioritize ethical decision-making, several benefits emerge:

1. **Enhanced Stakeholder Trust and Confidence**: Ethical decisions demonstrate a commitment to integrity and accountability, which fosters trust and confidence among stakeholders. When stakeholders perceive that leaders are acting in the best interests of the organization and its constituents, they are more likely to trust the organization's leadership and remain supportive of its initiatives.

2. **Improved Reputation and Brand Image**: Ethical behavior enhances an organization's reputation and brand image. When leaders consistently make ethical decisions, they demonstrate the organization's commitment to upholding high standards of conduct and integrity. This positive reputation can attract customers, investors, and talent, creating long-term value for the organization.

3. **Stronger Relationships with Stakeholders**: Ethical decision-making builds stronger relationships with stakeholders, including customers, employees, suppliers, and communities. By considering the impact of their decisions on all stakeholders and acting with fairness and transparency, leaders cultivate trust and goodwill, which strengthens these relationships over time.

4. **Higher Employee Engagement and Retention**: Ethical leadership contributes to higher levels of employee engagement and retention. When employees perceive that their leaders are making ethical decisions and acting with integrity, they feel valued and respected. This sense of trust and fairness fosters a positive work environment where employees are more motivated, committed, and loyal to the organization.

5. **Greater Team Morale and Cohesion**: Ethical decisions positively impact team morale and cohesion. When leaders prioritize ethical behavior,

they create a culture of trust, respect, and accountability within the team. This fosters a sense of belonging and unity, where team members feel valued, supported, and empowered to contribute to the organization's success.

6. **Reduced Risk of Legal and Reputational Damage**: Ethical decision-making reduces the risk of legal and reputational damage for the organization. By adhering to ethical principles and values, leaders mitigate the likelihood of engaging in unethical or unlawful behavior that could result in legal consequences or reputational harm.

7. **Alignment with Organizational Values and Mission**: Ethical decisions align with the organization's values and mission, reinforcing its purpose and guiding principles. When leaders consistently make decisions that reflect these values, they strengthen the organization's culture and identity, fostering a sense of shared purpose and commitment among stakeholders.

Making ethical decisions as a leader has a positive impact on stakeholder interests and team morale by enhancing trust and confidence, improving reputation and brand image, strengthening relationships with stakeholders, increasing employee engagement and retention, fostering team morale and cohesion, reducing the risk of legal and reputational damage, and aligning with organizational values and mission. Ethical leadership is not only the right thing to do but also essential for building a sustainable and successful organization.

D. Your Role as an Ethical Leader

A leader's role as an ethical leader is akin to that of a beacon guiding a ship through tumultuous waters. Ethical leaders illuminate the path forward with unwavering integrity, compassion, and courage, inspiring those around them to reach new heights of excellence and righteousness.

Picture a leader who stands tall, not only in stature but also in moral fortitude. Their every action is a testament to their unwavering commitment to doing what is right, even when it's the most challenging path to tread. They lead by example, demonstrating to their team that ethics are not merely a set of rules to follow but a way of life—a compass guiding them through the complexities of decision-making.

An ethical leader embodies empathy, seeing beyond the surface to understand the hopes, fears, and aspirations of those they lead. They cultivate an environment of trust and inclusivity, where every voice is heard, and every opinion matters.

Courage is the hallmark of ethical leadership. In the face of adversity, ethical leaders stand firm, unwavering in their commitment to uphold principles of fairness, justice, and integrity. They do not shy away from difficult decisions or uncomfortable conversations but confront challenges head-on with grace and determination. It is this courage that emboldens others to follow suit, to rise above their own fears and doubts, and to strive for excellence in all they do.

But perhaps most importantly, **an ethical leader is a beacon of hope in a world often marred by cynicism and distrust.** They remind us that goodness still exists—that even in the darkest of times, there are those who will stand up for what is right and just. Through their actions and their words, they inspire us to believe in ourselves, in each other, and in the limitless potential of humanity to create a better world.

In essence, a leader's role as an ethical leader is to be a guiding light—a source of inspiration and guidance for all who have the privilege of following in their footsteps. **They lead not with fear or coercion but with love, empathy, and unwavering integrity.** They remind us that true greatness is not measured by wealth, power, or status but by the depth of one's character and the impact they have on the lives of others. And in doing so, they leave an indelible mark on the world—a legacy of kindness, compassion, and unwavering moral courage that will endure for generations to come.

A leader often cited for their ethical leadership is Nelson Mandela. As the anti-apartheid revolutionary and former President of South Africa, Mandela exemplified moral courage, forgiveness, and reconciliation. Despite enduring 27 years of imprisonment for his opposition to apartheid, Mandela emerged as a symbol of hope and reconciliation, advocating for peace, equality, and human rights. He demonstrated ethical leadership by promoting inclusivity, tolerance, and forgiveness, overseeing the peaceful transition from apartheid to democracy in South Africa. Mandela's legacy as a moral leader and champion of justice continues to inspire ethical leadership and social change globally.

XII. Cultivating Leadership at Every Level

Organizations benefit significantly from cultivating leadership at every level, as it nurtures a workforce that is more engaged, adaptable, and empowered. Empowering employees to take on leadership roles fosters a culture of innovation and problem-solving, where individuals feel encouraged to contribute their ideas and take ownership of their work. This heightened engagement not only improves job satisfaction but also reduces turnover, as employees feel a stronger sense of fulfillment in their roles. Additionally, leadership at every level promotes collaboration and teamwork, breaking down silos and fostering a more cohesive organizational culture.

Furthermore, distributed leadership enhances the organization's adaptability and agility, enabling it to respond more effectively to changing market conditions and emerging opportunities. **By developing a pipeline of future leaders throughout the organization, companies ensure a steady supply of talent capable of driving innovation and growth in the long term.**

A. Delegating Authority and Encouraging Ownership

Empowerment and delegating authority play crucial roles in fostering ownership and accountability within a team or organization, from a leader's perspective. Here's how:

1. **Encourages Ownership**: When leaders empower their team members by delegating authority and granting them autonomy, individuals feel a sense of ownership over their work. They are more likely to take initiative, make decisions, and take responsibility for the outcomes,

knowing that they have the authority to act independently. This ownership mentality drives greater commitment and engagement among team members, as they feel personally invested in the success of their projects or initiatives.

2. **Fosters Accountability**: Empowerment goes hand in hand with accountability. When team members are given the authority to make decisions and act, they also bear the responsibility for the results. Leaders can hold individuals accountable for their performance and outcomes, knowing that they have been empowered to act autonomously. This accountability mindset promotes a culture of transparency, trust, and integrity within the team, where individuals hold themselves and each other to high standards of performance and conduct.

3. **Promotes Skill Development**: Delegating authority provides opportunities for team members to develop and hone their skills. When individuals are entrusted with decision-making responsibilities, they have the chance to learn from both their successes and failures, gaining valuable experience and expertise in the process. Leaders can support this skill development by providing guidance, feedback, and mentorship, helping team members grow into more capable and confident professionals.

4. **Increases Engagement and Motivation**: Empowerment and delegation empower team members to use their skills and expertise to make meaningful contributions to the organization. This sense of purpose and autonomy drives greater engagement and motivation, as individuals feel valued and respected for their abilities. When team members are empowered to take ownership of their work and make decisions that directly impact the outcomes, they are more likely to be motivated to perform at their best and strive for excellence.

5. **Drives Innovation and Creativity**: By empowering team members to make decisions and take initiative, leaders create an environment that encourages innovation and creativity. When individuals feel empowered to experiment, take risks, and explore new ideas, they are more likely to come up with innovative solutions to complex problems. Delegating authority allows leaders to tap into the diverse perspectives and talents of their team members, driving continuous improvement and driving organizational success.

Empowerment and delegating authority are essential tools for leaders to cultivate ownership and accountability within their teams. **By entrusting individuals with decision-making responsibilities, leaders foster a culture of ownership, accountability, skill development, engagement, and innovation, ultimately driving greater success and performance within the organization.**

B. Developing the Next Generation of Leaders

All of us leaders share the trait of ambition. Most successful leaders that I have known do not spend more than two to three years in their position before they expand their responsibilities and reach with higher level positions. We never want to leave our current teams stranded if we take on a promotion. For that reason, it is the duty and responsibility of a leader to mentor and coach their team, which is critical for developing the next generation of leaders. Here's a few ways how:

1. **Identifying Potential**: Leaders play a crucial role in identifying high-potential individuals within their team who have the drive, ambition, and potential to become future leaders. Through observation, assessment, and dialogue, leaders can identify team members who exhibit leadership qualities such as initiative, problem-solving skills, and the ability to influence others.

2. **Providing Guidance and Support**: Once potential leaders have been identified, it is the leader's responsibility to provide them with

guidance, support, and mentorship to help them develop their leadership skills. This includes offering advice, sharing experiences, and providing opportunities for growth and development. Leaders can act as role models and offer insights into effective leadership behaviors, communication strategies, and decision-making processes.

3. **Offering Feedback and Coaching**: Effective leaders provide ongoing feedback and coaching to help their team members grow and develop as leaders. This includes offering constructive feedback on performance, highlighting areas for improvement, and providing guidance on how to develop specific leadership competencies. Through regular coaching conversations, leaders can help individuals identify their strengths and weaknesses, set goals for improvement, and track their progress over time.

4. **Creating Development Opportunities**: Leaders have a responsibility to create opportunities for their team members to develop their leadership skills and gain hands-on experience. This may involve assigning challenging projects, offering stretch assignments, or providing opportunities for cross-functional collaboration. By exposing individuals to new challenges and experiences, leaders help them build confidence, resilience, and adaptability as future leaders.

5. **Encouraging Continuous Learning**: Leaders foster a culture of continuous learning and development within their team by encouraging individuals to seek out learning opportunities, pursue further education, and develop new skills. This may include providing access to training programs, workshops, seminars, and other resources to support ongoing growth and development. Leaders can also lead by example by investing in their own professional development and lifelong learning.

6. **Creating Succession Plans**: Leaders play a key role in succession planning by identifying potential successors for key leadership roles within the organization and developing plans to groom them for future leadership positions. This involves assessing the readiness and potential of potential successors, providing them with the necessary support and development opportunities, and creating pathways for advancement within the organization.

By providing guidance, support, feedback, and development opportunities, leaders empower their team members to grow and develop their leadership skills, ultimately ensuring the long-term success and sustainability of the organization.

C. Role Modeling the Behaviors You Want to See in Others

Leading by example is a fundamental aspect of effective leadership, where actions speak louder than words. By embodying the behaviors, values, and principles they wish to instill in their team members, leaders set a standard for excellence and inspire their teams to follow suit. Integrity and ethics form the cornerstone of leading by example, as leaders demonstrate honesty, fairness, and transparency in their actions and decisions. This fosters trust and respect among team members, who are more likely to emulate these ethical standards in their own work. **Leading by example promotes accountability and responsibility within the team, as leaders take ownership of their actions and hold themselves accountable for their performance.** This culture of accountability encourages team members to take pride in their work and strive for excellence, knowing that their efforts are valued and recognized.

Additionally, leading by example fosters collaboration and teamwork within the team, as leaders actively engage with their colleagues, listen to their perspectives, and value their contributions. By demonstrating openness and inclusivity, leaders create an environment where every team member feels empowered to share their ideas and work together towards common goals. Furthermore, leading by example encourages continuous learning and growth, as leaders demonstrate a growth mindset, a willingness to learn from failures, and a commitment to personal and professional development. This inspires team members to embrace opportunities for learning and growth, knowing that their leaders support and encourage their development.

Leading by example also inspires innovation and creativity within the team, as leaders encourage experimentation, risk-taking, and thinking outside the box. By fostering a culture of innovation, leaders empower their team members to explore new ideas and solutions, driving creativity and driving the organization forward.

Leading by example serves as a powerful tool for effective leadership, as it demonstrates the behaviors, values, and principles that leaders want to see reflected in their team members. **By embodying integrity, ethics, accountability, collaboration, continuous learning, and innovation, leaders set a standard for excellence and inspire their teams to be successful.** Through their actions and decisions, leaders create a culture of excellence where every team member feels valued, respected, and empowered to achieve their full potential.

XIII.   Sustaining Leadership Excellence

Sustained leadership excellence is essential for the enduring success and resilience of an organization. Strong leadership provides strategic direction, ensuring alignment between organizational objectives and daily operations, which enables effective adaptation to changing market conditions. Leadership excellence also fosters a positive organizational culture based on shared values, trust, and accountability. This culture promotes employee engagement, productivity, and retention, driving organizational performance and growth.

Leadership excellence cultivates innovation and adaptability by empowering employees to challenge the status quo, explore new ideas, and drive continuous improvement. By fostering a culture of innovation, organizations can stay ahead of the competition and capitalize on emerging opportunities.

Additionally, sustained leadership excellence prioritizes talent development and succession planning. **Effective leaders invest in developing their teams, identifying high-potential employees, and preparing them for future leadership roles. This ensures a pipeline of capable leaders for the future, mitigating the risks associated with leadership turnover and ensuring continuity of leadership excellence over time.**

Furthermore, strong leadership excellence enhances stakeholder trust and reinforces the organization's reputation. By demonstrating transparency, integrity, and a commitment to corporate social responsibility, leaders build stronger relationships with customers, investors, employees, and communities, fostering trust and confidence in the organization's ability to deliver value and achieve its goals.

A. Investing in Your Development as a Leader

Investing time into leadership development is crucial for leaders to continuously improve and become stronger leaders than they are today for several reasons:

1. **Personal Growth**: Leadership development allows leaders to enhance their skills, knowledge, and abilities, leading to personal growth and self-improvement. By investing in their development, leaders can identify their strengths and weaknesses, set goals for improvement, and work towards becoming more effective leaders.

2. **Adaptability**: The business landscape is constantly evolving, with new challenges, technologies, and trends emerging regularly. Investing in leadership development enables leaders to stay agile and adaptable, equipping them with the skills and mindset needed to navigate change successfully. This adaptability allows leaders to lead their teams through uncertainty and drive organizational resilience.

3. **Enhanced Performance**: Strong leadership is essential for driving organizational performance and achieving strategic objectives. Leadership development helps leaders hone their leadership capabilities, enabling them to inspire and motivate their teams, make better decisions, and drive results. As leaders become more effective in their roles, they can positively impact employee engagement, productivity, and overall organizational success.

4. **Innovation and Creativity**: Strong leadership fosters a culture of innovation and creativity within the organization. Leadership development equips leaders with the skills to encourage innovation, promote collaboration, and foster a supportive environment where new ideas are welcomed and explored. By investing in their

development, leaders can inspire innovation and drive positive change within their teams and organizations.

Investing time into leadership development is essential for leaders to continuously improve and become stronger leaders than they are today. By focusing on personal growth, adaptability, enhanced performance, succession planning, and fostering innovation, leaders can position themselves and their organizations for long-term success in today's dynamic business environment.

B. Building a Leadership Development Plan

Building a leadership development plan is critical for a leader to become a stronger leader or someone aspiring to become a leader. Building this plan involves several key steps to set goals and priorities effectively, as follows:

1. **Self-Assessment**: Begin by conducting a thorough self-assessment to identify your current strengths, weaknesses, skills, and areas for improvement as a leader. Reflect on past experiences, feedback from colleagues and mentors, and any formal assessments or evaluations you've received.

2. **Define Goals and Priorities**: Based on your self-assessment, define specific, measurable, achievable, relevant, and time-bound (SMART) goals for your leadership development. Consider both short-term and long-term objectives, focusing on areas where you want to grow and improve as a leader.

3. **Identify Development Areas**: Identify specific areas for development that align with your goals and priorities. This could include enhancing communication skills, improving decision-making abilities, developing emotional intelligence, or honing strategic thinking capabilities.

4. **Research Development Opportunities**: Explore various development opportunities that can help you achieve your goals, such as workshops, training programs, coaching sessions, mentorship programs, online courses, or networking events. Consider both formal and informal learning opportunities that suit your learning style and schedule.

5. **Create an Action Plan**: Develop a detailed action plan outlining the steps you need to take to achieve your goals. Break down each goal into smaller, manageable tasks, and assign deadlines for completion. Prioritize your actions based on urgency and importance, focusing on high-impact activities that will drive meaningful progress.

6. **Monitor Progress and Adjust**: Regularly monitor your progress towards your goals and adjust as needed. Track your accomplishments, celebrate successes, and identify any obstacles or challenges that arise along the way. Be flexible and willing to adjust your plan as circumstances change or new opportunities arise.

7. **Seek Feedback and Support**: Solicit feedback from colleagues, mentors, and supervisors to gain insights into your progress and areas for improvement. Use this feedback to refine your development plan and make informed decisions about your leadership development journey.

8. **Reflect and Learn**: Take time to reflect on your experiences, lessons learned, and successes and failures throughout the development process. Use these reflections to continuously learn and grow as a leader, refining your skills and capabilities over time.

9. **Complacency**: Don't get stuck in your current position for too long. You never want to get promoted before you are ready but alternatively, you don't want to stay in the same position for too long either. If you

have high performance and have mastered your current performance metrics, it may be time to expand your influence on a larger audience. Hopefully the organization you work for will provide that opportunity, otherwise, you may be forced to look externally to continue your growth trajectory.

10. **Stay Committed and Motivated**: Finally, stay committed to your development plan and remain motivated to achieve your goals. Stay focused on your priorities, stay resilient in the face of setbacks, and stay open to new opportunities for growth and development. Remember that leadership development is a lifelong journey, and success comes from continuous learning and improvement.

This leadership development plan will be iterative as you execute it due to the dynamic nature of leadership development. As you engage in learning activities and gain new experiences, you'll inevitably encounter feedback, challenges, and changing circumstances that prompt you to reassess and adjust your approach. Feedback from colleagues, mentors, and your own reflections will provide valuable insights into your progress and areas for improvement, prompting revisions to your goals and action plan. This is something that you should share with your supervisor. They will appreciate your ambition and drive.

Ultimately, embracing an iterative approach enables you to continuously refine your skills, deepen your expertise, and evolve as a leader over time, ensuring your development remains relevant, effective, and aligned with your long-term goals.

C. Surround Yourself with Successful Mentors and Peers

Building a support network surrounded by mentors and peers is crucial for a leader's development for several reasons:

1. **Access to Diverse Perspectives**: Mentors and peers offer different perspectives and insights based on their experiences and expertise. Engaging with individuals from diverse backgrounds and industries

allows leaders to gain new insights, challenge their assumptions, and broaden their horizons, enhancing their problem-solving abilities and decision-making skills.

2. **Guidance and Advice**: Mentors provide guidance, advice, and wisdom based on their own leadership journeys and experiences. They can offer valuable insights into navigating challenges, seizing opportunities, and developing leadership competencies, helping leaders navigate their career paths with confidence and clarity.

3. **Accountability and Support**: A support network of mentors and peers provides accountability and support, helping leaders stay motivated and focused on their development goals. Peers can offer encouragement, share resources, and provide emotional support during challenging times, fostering a sense of camaraderie, and belonging.

4. **Learning and Growth Opportunities**: Interacting with mentors and peers exposes leaders to new ideas, best practices, and emerging trends in leadership and management. Collaborating on projects, participating in peer learning groups, and attending networking events provide opportunities for continuous learning and professional growth, enabling leaders to stay relevant and competitive in their fields.

5. **Professional Networking**: Building relationships with mentors and peers expands a leader's professional network, opening doors to new opportunities for collaboration, career advancement, and personal development. Networking with individuals in different industries and roles increases visibility, enhances credibility, and facilitates career progression through referrals and introductions.

6. **Role Modeling and Inspiration**: Mentors serve as role models and sources of inspiration for leaders, demonstrating leadership excellence and providing a roadmap for success. Observing the behaviors, strategies, and habits of successful mentors can inspire leaders to emulate their best practices and strive for excellence in their own leadership journey.

Building a support network surrounded by mentors and peers is essential for a leader's development. Mentors provide guidance, advice, and wisdom, while peers offer diverse perspectives, accountability, and support. Engaging with this network fosters continuous learning, growth, and professional networking opportunities, empowering leaders to navigate challenges, seize opportunities, and achieve their full potential.

D. Seeking Feedback and Mentoring

Seeking feedback from peers and supervisors is a fundamental aspect of leadership development, serving as a catalyst for growth and improvement. Leaders who actively seek input from those around them gain valuable insights into their performance, strengths, and areas for development. Peers and supervisors can offer diverse perspectives, drawing attention to blind spots that may hinder leadership effectiveness. **By understanding how your actions and behaviors are perceived by others, leaders can make targeted adjustments to their approach, communication style, and decision-making processes.**

Seeking feedback also fosters a culture of accountability and continuous improvement within the organization. **Leaders who demonstrate a willingness to listen and learn inspire trust and confidence among their teams, encouraging open dialogue and constructive feedback.** This creates a supportive environment where individuals feel empowered to share their insights and ideas, driving innovation and collaboration. Additionally, leaders who actively seek feedback demonstrate humility and a commitment to personal and professional growth, setting an example for their teams to follow.

Furthermore, feedback serves as a valuable learning tool, accelerating the development process for leaders. Rather than relying solely on self-assessment or trial and error, leaders can leverage the experiences and perspectives of others to identify areas of strength and opportunities for growth more quickly. This enables leaders to make informed decisions and progress more rapidly in their development journey.

Finally, seeking feedback strengthens relationships and fosters trust within the organization. **When leaders demonstrate a genuine interest in understanding and addressing the concerns and perspectives of their peers and supervisors, it builds rapport and creates a sense of camaraderie.** This trust and respect form the foundation for effective collaboration and teamwork, leading to improved performance and results.

Feedback from peers and supervisors is essential for leadership development. It provides valuable insights, fosters a culture of accountability and continuous improvement, accelerates learning, and strengthens relationships within the organization. By embracing feedback as a catalyst for growth and improvement, leaders can enhance their effectiveness and drive positive change in their teams and organizations.

XIV.   Leaving a Legacy

To lead for impact and create a lasting legacy, leaders can implement several key strategies. Firstly, they must articulate a clear vision that inspires others and outlines the impact the organization aims to achieve. Setting ambitious yet achievable goals aligned with this vision ensures that efforts are focused and purposeful. Empowering others through delegation, trust, and accountability amplifies the leader's impact, fostering a culture of ownership and engagement throughout the organization. Leading with integrity, upholding high ethical standards, and prioritizing people development build trust and credibility, laying the foundation for a sustainable legacy of ethical leadership.

Additionally, driving innovation and embracing change within the organization fosters transformative impact, leaving a legacy of progress and adaptability in the face of evolving challenges. Leaders should also regularly measure progress, celebrate successes, and actively contribute to the development of future leaders. By mentoring, supporting community initiatives, and championing causes aligned with the organization's values, leaders can leave a positive and lasting impact that extends far beyond their tenure.

Ultimately, **leading for impact requires a commitment to driving meaningful change, optimal business results, empowering others, and leaving a legacy that inspires and shapes the future for the better.** Through these strategies, leaders can ensure that their influence endures long after they have moved on, leaving a legacy of purpose, progress, and positive change in their wake.

A. The Power of Purpose-Driven Leadership

Purpose-driven leadership can have a profound and positive impact on an organization in several ways. Firstly, it inspires and motivates employees by providing them with a clear sense of purpose and direction. **When leaders articulate a compelling purpose that goes beyond profit and resonates with the values and aspirations of employees, it fosters a sense of meaning and fulfillment in their work.** This, in turn, leads to higher levels of engagement, productivity, and commitment to the organization's goals.

Purpose-driven leadership also aligns employees around a common cause, fostering collaboration and unity of effort. **When everyone in the organization is working towards a shared purpose, it breaks down silos, encourages teamwork, and promotes a culture of cooperation.** This collaborative environment enables employees to leverage their diverse skills and perspectives to overcome challenges and drive innovation.

Organizational resilience and adaptability is also positively affected by purpose-driven leadership. In times of uncertainty or change, a strong sense of purpose provides employees with a guiding light, helping them navigate challenges and stay focused on what truly matters. Leaders who lead with purpose are better equipped to make strategic decisions that align with the organization's long-term objectives, even in the face of adversity.

Additionally, **purpose-driven leadership strengthens the organization's brand and reputation.** When leaders authentically embody the organization's purpose and values, it creates trust and credibility with customers, investors, and other stakeholders. Organizations that are perceived as purpose-driven are more attractive to customers, more resilient in times of crisis, and more appealing to top talent.

Furthermore, purpose-driven leadership contributes to societal impact and sustainability. Leaders who prioritize purpose over profit are more likely to consider the broader social and environmental implications of their decisions. By aligning business objectives with societal needs and environmental stewardship, purpose-driven organizations can create positive change in the world while also driving business success.

A purpose-driven leader has the power to transform organizations by inspiring employees, fostering collaboration, enhancing resilience, strengthening the brand, and driving positive societal impact.

B. Impact of Advocacy in your community and how it Affects Your Companies Reputation

Being involved in advocacy within the community is essential for leaders as it underscores their commitment to social responsibility and making a meaningful impact beyond their business operations. Advocacy provides a platform for leaders to actively engage with key stakeholders, including local government officials, nonprofit organizations, and community leaders, fostering collaboration and mutual support. **By participating in advocacy initiatives, leaders can build valuable relationships that not only enhance the company's brand image and reputation but also create opportunities for partnership and innovation.**

Furthermore, advocacy allows leaders to demonstrate their values and principles, aligning their actions with the company's mission and vision. When leaders advocate for causes that resonate with their stakeholders, they strengthen the connection between the company and its community, building trust and credibility. This can have a significant impact on the company's reputation, as customers, employees, and other stakeholders are more likely to view the company positively when they see its leaders actively working to address important social and environmental issues.

Being involved in advocacy helps leaders stay informed about important social, environmental, and regulatory issues that may impact the company's operations. **By staying ahead of emerging trends and developments, leaders can proactively address risks and opportunities, ensuring the company remains competitive and resilient in a rapidly changing landscape.** This proactive approach to advocacy not only mitigates potential risks but also drives innovation within the company, as leaders seek creative solutions to address societal challenges while advancing their business objectives.

Additionally, advocacy can play a crucial role in talent attraction and retention, particularly among younger generations who prioritize corporate social responsibility. Millennials and Gen Z are more likely to be drawn to companies that demonstrate a commitment to social causes and are actively engaged in advocacy and community initiatives. By aligning their advocacy efforts with the values and interests of these younger generations, leaders can attract and retain top talent who share similar values and aspirations.

Being involved in advocacy within the community is not only a reflection of a leader's commitment to social responsibility but also a strategic imperative for building trust, credibility, and long-term success. By actively engaging in advocacy initiatives, leaders can strengthen relationships, enhance the company's reputation, drive innovation, and attract top talent, ultimately contributing to a positive impact on both the company and the community it serves.

C. Unleash the Leader Within You

Leadership, viewed from the perspective of unleashing the leader within, emphasizes the innate potential within everyone to lead and make a positive impact. This approach rejects the notion that leadership is confined to a select few and instead recognizes that leadership is a mindset and a set of skills that can be developed and cultivated by anyone. Unleashing the leader within involves tapping into one's strengths, values, and passions to inspire and influence others, regardless of formal authority or position.

At its core, unleashing the leader within is about self-awareness and authenticity. It begins with a deep understanding of one's strengths, weaknesses, values, and purpose. By knowing oneself, individuals can confidently embrace their unique qualities and lead from a place of authenticity, rather than trying to conform to traditional leadership stereotypes. This authenticity not only fosters trust and credibility but also inspires others to do the same, creating a culture of openness and collaboration.

Unleashing the leader within involves developing key leadership skills, such as communication, empathy, resilience, and adaptability. These skills enable individuals to effectively navigate challenges, inspire others, and drive positive change. **Rather than waiting for opportunities to arise, individuals** who unleash the leader within actively seek out ways to make a difference and drive impact, whether it's within their team, organization, or community regardless of their current title.

Importantly, unleashing the leader within is not limited to formal leadership roles or titles. It can manifest in various aspects of life, from leading a team project at work to volunteering in the local community. By recognizing that leadership is not bound by hierarchy or authority, individuals can embrace opportunities to lead in whatever context they find themselves in, leveraging their unique strengths and perspectives to drive meaningful change.

Furthermore, unleashing the leader within involves a continuous journey of growth and development. It requires individuals to adopt a growth mindset, embrace feedback, and be willing to learn and adapt over time. By committing to ongoing personal and professional development, individuals can unlock their full potential as leaders and create lasting impact in the world around them.

In essence, leadership from the perspective of unleashing the leader within empowers individuals to recognize and embrace their innate leadership potential, regardless of their background or circumstances.

D. Speaking to the masses

Public speaking is an indispensable skill for successful business leaders, playing a pivotal role in their ability to communicate effectively, inspire others, and drive organizational success. In today's fast-paced and interconnected business environment, leaders must be adept at conveying their ideas, vision, and strategy to a wide range of stakeholders, including employees, investors, customers, and the public. Public speaking enables leaders to engage with audiences, articulate their message clearly, and influence perceptions and behaviors. It also **provides a platform for leaders to demonstrate their expertise, thought leadership, and credibility, establishing them as authoritative figures in their respective fields.**

One of the primary reasons why public speaking is essential for business leaders is its role in effective communication. Business leaders are tasked with conveying complex ideas, strategies, and plans to diverse audiences with varying levels of knowledge and understanding. Public speaking allows them to distill complex concepts into clear and concise messages that resonate with their audience. **Whether addressing employees at a company-wide meeting, delivering a keynote presentation at a conference, or pitching to potential investors, leaders must be able to communicate their ideas persuasively and compellingly to achieve their objectives.**

It is also a powerful tool for inspiring and motivating others. Successful leaders often use their platform to share their vision, values, and passion for their work, inspiring others to share in their enthusiasm and commitment. By sharing personal anecdotes, experiences, and insights, leaders can connect with their audience on an emotional level, fostering trust, loyalty, and engagement. Effective public speaking enables leaders to rally support for their initiatives, mobilize teams towards common goals, and cultivate a culture of innovation, collaboration, and excellence within their organizations.

Public speaking also enhances a leader's credibility and reputation. When leaders deliver articulate and compelling presentations, they demonstrate their expertise, knowledge, and confidence in their subject matter. This builds trust and confidence among stakeholders, positioning leaders as credible and authoritative sources of information and guidance. It also helps leaders to establish their personal brand and differentiate themselves from their peers in the industry. As leaders consistently deliver engaging and impactful presentations, they become recognized as thought leaders and influencers within their respective fields.

A successful leader will be given opportunities to showcase their leadership skills and showcase their organization's achievements and capabilities. Whether speaking at industry conferences, investor meetings, or media interviews, leaders can use public speaking engagements to highlight their organization's successes, innovation, and strategic direction. By effectively communicating their organization's value proposition and competitive advantage, leaders can attract new customers, investors, and business partners, driving growth and expansion opportunities.

Speaking in public provides leaders a platform for networking and relationship-building. Business leaders often participate in speaking engagements at industry events, conferences, and seminars, where they can connect with peers, industry experts, potential partners, and customers. These interactions enable leaders to establish valuable connections, exchange ideas, and explore collaboration opportunities that can benefit their organization. These speaking engagements allow leaders to raise their profile within their industry, positioning themselves and their organization as thought leaders and influencers.

Speaking to the masses is a critical skill for successful business leaders, enabling them to communicate effectively, inspire others, and drive organizational success. **By mastering the art of public speaking, leaders can convey their ideas, vision, and strategy with clarity and conviction, inspire trust and confidence among stakeholders, and establish themselves as credible and authoritative figures in their respective fields.**

XV. Conclusion

Throughout this book we have explored the dynamic and diverse landscape of leadership, challenging the conventional notion that leadership is one-dimensional and uniform. Throughout this journey, we discovered that true leadership is not about conforming to a predefined mold but rather about embracing the unique qualities and strengths that reside within everyone. **By recognizing that leadership is a deeply personal and multifaceted journey, we've unlocked the potential for anyone, regardless of background or circumstance, to become a leader within their own right.**

A. Final Thoughts on the Dynamic Nature of Leadership

The dynamic nature of leadership underscores its responsiveness to the ever-changing landscape of organizations, markets, and society. Strong leaders are indispensable in this context, as they possess the agility, vision, and skills to navigate complexity and drive organizational success. Adaptability is paramount, enabling leaders to pivot strategies, embrace innovation, and effectively manage change. A strong leader's strategic vision provides clarity and direction, inspiring employees and aligning efforts towards common goals. Effective communication is essential for building trust, fostering collaboration, and ensuring everyone is aligned with organizational objectives.

Furthermore, strong leaders prioritize talent development, nurturing the growth and potential of their team members to build a resilient workforce. During times of change or crisis, strong leaders provide stability, make informed decisions, and communicate transparently to manage uncertainty. Upholding ethical standards is foundational, as strong leaders lead by example, fostering a culture of integrity, trust, and accountability. In essence, strong leaders play a pivotal role in navigating the dynamic landscape of leadership, driving innovation, resilience, and ethical excellence within organizations.

B. Empowering Readers to Embrace Their Leadership Journey

To all leaders on their unique journey: Your path as a leader is as diverse as the experiences and perspectives that shape it. Embrace this journey with confidence and conviction, knowing that your individuality is your greatest asset. Your unique blend of strengths, values, and insights has the power to make a meaningful difference in the world.

As you navigate the challenges and opportunities that come your way, remember to lead with authenticity and purpose. Be true to yourself, honoring your values and beliefs as you inspire and empower those around you. Your authenticity will resonate, fostering trust, respect, and loyalty.

Embrace the opportunity to make a positive impact on the lives of others. Whether you lead a team, an organization, or a community, your actions have the potential to create ripple effects that extend far beyond your immediate sphere of influence. Approach each day with a sense of purpose and intentionality, seeking out opportunities to uplift and support those in need.

Commit to lifelong learning, seeking out new experiences and perspectives that challenge and inspire you. Embrace feedback as a gift, using it to refine your leadership approach and become the best version of yourself.

Embrace your unique leadership journey, knowing that you have the power to create positive change and leave a lasting legacy of impact and inspiration. The world is waiting for your leadership, so go forth with courage, compassion, and determination, and make your mark on the world.

Above all, remember that Leadership is not about job titles or social status, and it is definitely NOT one size fits all—it's about being selfless and making a difference in the lives of others. People follow people, People *will* follow you!

About the Author

Nico D'Alessandro wrote *People Follow Me: Unlocking Effective Leadership* along with *People Buy from Me: A Comprehensive Guide to Growing Sales by Building Lasting Connections with your Customers* to provide the foundational steps to building, growing, and leveraging customer relationships in leadership and sales.

Nico graduated from the School of Mines in Golden, CO in 2002 with a Bachelor of Science in Engineering. After 6 years of engineering consulting, heavily associated in the housing industry, he was laid off. This of course coincides with the 2008-2009 financial crisis. This unfortunate event also coincided with the birth of his first child, Antonio. No pressure, but it was essential to his family's wellbeing that he finds work. Thankfully, the support group from his lifelong friends from college went into full effect. One of his fraternity brothers was working at Siemens (large global corporation) as a HVAC service salesperson. Special thanks to Travis Fletcher for helping to ask around and Payman Farrokyhar for convincing the sales manager at Siemens to give him a shot.

Nico didn't have any traditional sales experience. He was however very social and played college soccer. Being around sports his entire life taught him values that he took into his career. Leadership came naturally to him, which came across during the interview. He was offered an entry level sales position in early 2009.

Even though speaking to people and being social was second nature, sales did not come easily is his first year. He took a very technical approach to sales and assumed that the more he estimated, the more he would sell. In theory, that makes sense. In the real world, that couldn't be further from the truth. He started halfway through the Siemens fiscal year, but only attained 5% of his sales quota at the end of that year. Thankfully he was in the year of forgiveness, but he knew the hall pass wouldn't last forever. That is when he made one of the best decisions of his career. He decided to estimate half the projects he typically would and push himself out of his cubicle to spend time with customers. He wasn't an expert in sales or HVAC, but he had 'the gift of gab'. He could talk to just about anyone about anything. What he lacked in experience he made up for with great communication and a high emotional intelligence.

      Nico started spending as much time with the customers that would be willing to spend time with him. He asked a lot of questions and bought a lot of lunches and rounds of golf. The goal was not to just spend company money on entertaining customers, but to lower their guards long enough, to understand what they needed and the kind of people they were. Relationships are not built overnight, and customers are often skeptical of your intentions. He spent a lot of time getting to know them. He was rewarded with their business, eventually. For some it was a few months, for others it took years. The journey to trust and business has no defined timeline, but with effort and great communication, that timeline was shortened.

      Nico entered the technical sales industry in 2009. After 5 years as a seller he became a local market sales manager, then a regional sales manager, then a National sales managers, then a General manager spending 2-3 years in each position before expanding his role to a new one. He currently serves as a sales leader, mentor and coach to other sales and General managers on sales leadership and market growth in the Western US for a Fortune 100 company. He and his family reside in beautiful San Diego, California.

Please connect with me at by searching for "People Buy from Me" on LinkedIn:

www.linkedin.com/in/nicolas-dalessandro-People-Buy-from-Me

or email me at:

peoplebuyfromme@gmail.com

I would love to hear from you with your feedback, successes, testimonials, comments, or suggestions. I wish you the absolute best in your leadership journey.

All the best,

Nico D'Alessandro

www.ingramcontent.com/pod-product-compliance
Lightning Source LLC
Chambersburg PA
CBHW050304230526
45471CB00005B/2006